THE COMPLETE
BAG MAKING
Masterclass

THE COMPLETE
BAG MAKING
Masterclass

The Comprehensive
Guide to Modern Bag
Making Techniques

Samantha Hussey

DAVID & CHARLES

www.davidandcharles.com

Contents

Foreword

When I was approached to write the foreword for this book, my initial reaction was one of slight fear – not over whether I could have enough wonderful things to say about Samantha's character and knowledge, but whether I could express myself well enough to give her and this book the credit they deserve. It's a complete honour to be able to write this for the author, Samantha Hussey, whom I consider one of my dearest friends.

Samantha and I met through a joint project, The Bag of the Month Club, a pattern subscription club started by several popular bag pattern designers. Although I live in Canada and Samantha in Wales, we had an instant connection and friendship that has been one of support, laughter and guidance. Communicating online has been a daily part of our lives since 2014, and I think we both cherish the opportunity to laugh and vent about our day, as well as provide each other with feedback and support for our design process and 'work life'. There were times during the earlier years of my business when each of us was sewing or administrating alone, but my work life didn't feel like a solitary event because I always had a colleague in Samantha. Her skill and design support has been invaluable to me, and I know that if I need to call on her to help me solve a construction issue, or if I just need someone to listen, she will always be there. I am always amazed at how she sees shapes and 3D construction, and then can put it all together on paper in a way that is easy to understand.

I was thrilled to be able to attend her bag making retreats in Wales twice, and stayed at her home with her beautiful family. Those trips were the absolute best trips I have ever had. During that time, I was able to see Samantha's teaching ability in action. She can have a group of people with different skill levels in a large room, sewing to their hearts content, and everyone who needs help gets help and everyone walks away pleased with their beautiful projects!

This book has the core skills at the front, teaching you all of the good stuff in an easy-to-follow way, plus tons of additional tips. Read through the skills and then jump into the projects, starting with the simplest and moving on to the more difficult ones. Samantha has provided you with the techniques to be successful as if you were right there in the room with her. Her natural ability to teach shines through the pages, and combined with awesome photography to accompany the instructions, we can all feel as if we are learning from Samantha in person.

I am so fortunate to call Samantha my friend and I could not be more proud of her. This is one of the most useful bag making books available, and sure to be one you will refer to over and over again. Well done, Samantha!

Janelle MacKay

J MacKay ♡

Emmaline Bags Inc.

Introduction

Thank you for picking up this book; it has been an absolute pleasure to write. I've packed it full of as much as I can about contemporary and structured bag making so that you can use it to help you make any pattern from any designer.

At the front of the book you'll find a wealth of information on tools, materials and up-to-date techniques, with added tips and tricks to make your bag making journey easier and more satisfying.

Following the techniques section are eight projects for you to put your new skills into action. You can customize any of these patterns using the techniques in the front section – adding pockets, hardware, customizing straps or even resizing the bag to suit your own needs. The projects range from beginner level to advanced; you can work through them in order, or select whichever bag you most like the look of and modify it to suit your skill level. You could, for example, add a zipped divider to the beginner-level Piped Hobo for an extra challenge, or you could leave out the zipped closure and the interior pockets of the Criss-Cross Shoulder Bag for a more beginner-friendly structured bag with the same look.

The best part of bag making is surely having a bag that's perfect for your needs and this book contains everything you need to know to be able to achieve this. I hope you enjoy *The Complete Bag Making Masterclass* and join the ranks of 'bagineers' all over the world.

I can't wait to see what you make!

Mrs H

Tools & Materials

TOOLS

Here are some of the tools you'll need to make structured bags. Some of them you may already have from previous projects; others are specific to the materials you'll be using and may be worth investing in as you progress in your bag making journey.

1 ROTARY CUTTER AND RULER
Useful for cutting rectangles and squares quickly and for trimming up edges after applying stabilizer.

2 THREAD SNIPS
These make quick work of cutting off loose thread ends.

3–4 LARGE AND SMALL SHARP SCISSORS
Useful for cutting out, notching, clipping seams and trimming away seam allowances to reduce bulk.

5 PAPER SCISSORS
Great for cutting out pattern pieces, and for cutting foam, plastic tubing and anything other than fabric.

6 PINKING SHEARS
Use to trim around curves to reduce bulk in the seam allowances. Trim using pinking shears instead of notching curves for a quick finish.

7–8 STEAM IRON AND PRESSING CLOTH
Essential for a professional finish; steam press the seams of your bag as you sew and use a pressing cloth for delicate areas such as zips and the edges of vinyl.

9 SEAM GAUGE
Especially useful for smaller seam allowances or instances where accuracy is key.

10 HERA MARKER
Use to score along fabric to ensure a crisp fold, ideal for card slots and for marking in visible areas.

11–12 SEAM RIPPER AND SHARP CRAFT KNIFE
Both can be used to cut slits for hardware prongs and turning gaps for zip pockets.

13 BODKIN
Use to thread elastic through pocket channels.

14 GOOD-QUALITY FABRIC GLUE
Ideal for holding zips in place and for securing hardware in place alongside the fitting screws.

15 ROTATING HOLE PUNCH
Ideal for making guide holes without disturbing the neighbours!

16–19 HAMMER, RIVET SETTER, HOLE PUNCH AND ANVIL
Use on a solid surface with an old chopping board for protection (*see Hardware & Bling: Rivets*).

20 TAILOR'S CLAPPER
The tailor's clapper is a must-have for pressing faux leather and cork, which can't usually be pressed on directly.

21 MARKING TOOLS
Use a pencil for marking zip boxes and hardware placement on interfacing; use chalk markers that can be easily removed for marking placements on visible areas.

22 MINI DUCT TAPE
To protect sharp hardware backs from wearing through fabrics, add a piece of mini duct tape to the back of hardware once it's installed.

23 WASH-AWAY DOUBLE-SIDED BASTING TAPE
This is usually 6mm (¼in) wide, which is ideal for bag making, and won't gum up the needle. Use it to hold zips in place to ensure accurate stitching.

24 CROCHET HOOK
Perfect for running along the inside of seams to ensure pockets are turned out fully, into corners to keep them sharp and around flap curves to encourage a good rounded edge.

25 SET OF SMALL SCREWDRIVERS
Ideally magnetic, in cross-slot sizes 00–1 and plain slot 2–3mm. Perfect for fitting hardware.

26 AWL
Ideal for making guide holes for hardware and helping to feed thick, bulky fabrics through the sewing machine.

27 FRAY CHECK
Use on any holes punched into fabric for rivets, hardware, fastenings and also on any seams clipped a tad too close to the stitching. Choose one that dries clear.

28 GLASS-HEADED PINS
Steam is so important in bag making that it's best not to risk melting pin heads!

29 QUILTING CLIPS
Far better for holding bulky fabrics together than pins; bulldog clips and laundry pegs also work well.

30 TAPE MEASURE
This is essential for accurate measuring.

31 MINI FLUSH RIVET CUTTERS
For those accidental moments when you need to remove a rivet.

32 STAPLER
Use this to secure the bases of bags in place by stapling well within the seam allowance. Once sewn, you can trim away the seam allowance and staples. It ensures no shifting!

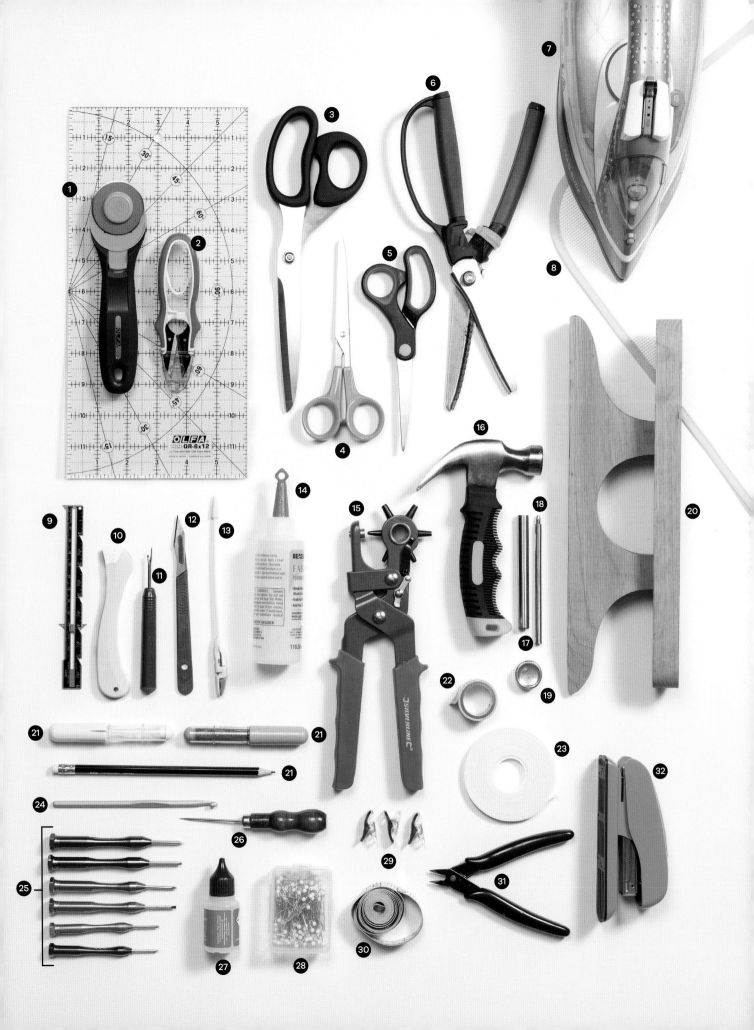

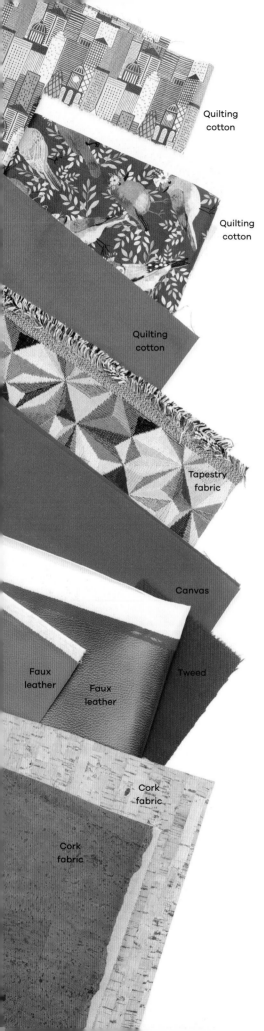

Quilting
cotton

Quilting
cotton

Quilting
cotton

Tapestry
fabric

Canvas

Faux
leather

Faux
leather

Tweed

Cork
fabric

Cork
fabric

FABRICS

With the ever-improving technologies available in fabric making today, you don't have to limit yourself to using quilting cottons for your bags. Although it can look fantastic, sometimes you may want to add a bit of variety and mix & match materials. Listed below are some of the most popular materials for bag making – but if you'd like to use a gorgeous piece of silk or some stretchy fun jersey, you can do so by adding some interfacing until it has the stability required.

QUILTING COTTON

Quilting cotton is a great option for bag making – it folds well, is easy to sew and comes in a wide variety of fun prints. Try to buy good-quality cotton to prevent colour transfer. *See Professional Touches: Preparing the Fabric* for advice on preparing to sew cotton.

CANVAS AND TAPESTRY FABRIC

Canvas can give bags more of a utility look, whereas tapestry fabric provides a very structured finish. They both work well on larger bags that benefit from added form. Be prepared to apply interfacing right up to the edges to prevent fraying and apply Fray Check to any holes punched for rivets and hardware.

TWEEDS AND WOOLS

Tweeds and wools work so well for bag making, often giving a heritage feel. It's a good idea to pre-steam tweeds and wools before you cut them out, as they can shrink a little. There's no need to pre-wash them, but ensure any shrinking is done before cutting. It's also a good idea to apply interfacing right up to the edges to prevent the fabric from stretching or the edges from fraying, regardless of the thickness of the wool. Use a tailor's clapper to set seams to prevent scorching on tweed and wool fabrics.

FAUX LEATHER

Faux leather comes in a vast array of colours and is easy to sew on most domestic sewing machines. It works best on rounded bags if your machine isn't particularly strong, although if your machine can handle it, boxed corner-style bags work well, too. Remember not to use pins, as they'll leave marks, and keep pressing to a minimum to avoid the fabric melting. If you do need to unpick, try holding the seam under a hair dryer for a few seconds to minimize any holes left behind.

CORK

Cork fabric, sometimes called cork leather, is a great alternative to faux leather. It's naturally waterproof and lightweight to carry. You will not usually need to apply interfacing and may choose to use a fusible fleece rather than a foam stabilizer. Treat as faux leather but be aware that, over time, any sharp corners such as boxed corners can result in the cork wearing away from the backing. It's ideal for rounder shapes.

INTERFACING AND STABILIZERS

The main difference between interfacing and stabilizers is that interfacing strengthens while stabilizers add body. Interface fabrics that you wish to add pockets to, or straps or anything that you'd like to prevent from fraying or stretching.

INTERFACING

Fusible interfacing is best and there are two options with a medium-weight interfacing: woven and non woven. A woven interfacing is one that has defined warp and weft threads and has a stretch across the bias. Generally, you should cut woven interfacing on the grain to minimize stretch, although this can result in more wastage. Woven interfacing provides a natural feel to any fabric that it is applied to and has a lovely soft drape.

Alternatively you could opt for a non-woven interfacing, which is around half the price of woven and has no defined grain line. It can feel a little flimsy and tear easily before it is applied, but once fused to the fabric it creates a crisp, slightly firm feel. The fabric feels slightly papery once it is applied, but pockets and seam lines are often crisper and more defined with this finish.

Many of my testers prefer to use woven interfacing on their bag exteriors to provide a natural, softer feel on the outside, but find that a non-woven interfacing is best for linings as the linings sit more neatly once the bag is fully constructed. Many stores offer samples of both types, so it can be useful to fuse a sample to your chosen fabric to decide which finish you prefer.

STABILIZERS

The type of stabilizer you choose will depend on the bag you are making. The three main stabilizers that I use for bag making are a fusible high-loft fleece, a sew-in foam and an ultra-firm fusible.

Fusible high-loft fleece is ideal for a softer bag finish such as a hobo bag or a slouchy-style bag. It's also good for flaps, where you may not want such a firm finish, and on smaller bags and pouches where too much stabilizer would make the bag impractical to use. Fusible fleece can be cut smaller than the main bag panels to reduce bulk in the seams, as it will remain in place once fused to the fabric. Fusible fleece adds substance to a bag but does not usually result in a bag that is able to stand on its own, except in smaller bags.

Sew-in foam stabilizer is possibly the most commonly used stabilizer for structured bags. Foams are readily available now and come with either a knitted finish either side of the foam or a felted finish. Foams with a knitted finish tend to be easier to sew for those without powerful sewing machines, but felted finish foams are usually lower in price and come in wider options. Both will provide a great structured finish to a bag, but steer clear of fusible foams in larger bags, as it's very hard to prevent unsightly wrinkles!

To apply a foam stabilizer, first add any interfacing to the exterior main panels of a bag, then smooth the fabric over the foam, pinning in opposite corners to ensure a taut finish. If you're using faux leather as the exterior fabric, pin inside the seam allowance. Tack (baste) around the edge of the main panels, using a seam allowance slightly smaller than that of the bag you are sewing. (For example, for a bag with a 1cm (⅜in) seam allowance, tack the foam 6mm (¼in) from the edge.

After tacking, trim the excess foam from the seam allowance. This will help the finished seams sit neatly and reduce bulk going through your sewing machine.

For bags with boxed corners, it's really helpful to trim away an extra 1.2cm (½in) from around each boxed corner and in each top corner to reduce thickness for a bag's final construction. A little extra time and effort spent applying stabilizers at the start really does make a big difference to a finished bag.

The third kind of stabilizer that you will find useful in your bag making is an ultra-firm stabilizer such as fusible Decovil 1 or Peltex. This product, when fused to quilting cotton, can result in a fabric that has the hand of leather. It is ideal for clutch bags, wallets or any small structured bag. It's not the cheapest product on the market but is well worth the price, as you don't need much for it to make a big difference. Try not to sew over it: it's incredibly thick to sew through. It fuses well, so cut it well within the seam allowance. For a bag with a 1cm (⅜in) seam allowance, it's best to trim the ultra-firm stabilizer 1.2cm (½in) smaller on all sides, so that there's no risk of it being caught in any stitching. It's also handy for fusing onto the bottom of bags where you don't want to add a rigid base and feet but would like a little extra stability.

Fusible fleece

Foam stabilizer

Decovil 1

Woven interfacing

NEEDLES

Ideally you should change your needle every six hours of sewing; I like to change mine each time I start a new bag. Buy the sizes you use the most in bulk, as a sharp needle really makes a big difference in neat topstitching and preventing threads from shredding as you sew.

Needle sizes usually have two numbers – a European size and a US size. The most common sizes for bag making are #80 and #100 (US 12 and 16).

For linings, it's best to use a #70 or #80 (US 11 or 12). A good-quality universal needle is sufficient. For exteriors and heavier fabrics, a #90 or #100 (US 14 or 16) is perfect. These larger needles pierce the fabric more easily without the risk of bending.

Good-quality needles are designed to shatter if they meet any resistance in order to protect the sewing machine, but try not to force anything bulky through your machine. If a needle breaks while you are sewing, make sure you retrieve all of the broken pieces and check for burrs in your needle plate and bobbin case; these can usually be filed out by a sewing-machine repairer.

A universal needle is a great all-rounder for bag making, but if you find you are not producing neat stitches you could try one of the following needles.

Jeans needles usually come in the larger sizes and are ideal for fabrics with a heavy woven finish, such as canvas, denim or twill. The blade is reinforced and has a ballpoint tip that moves the threads of the fabric as you sew rather than having to pierce the fabric.

Topstitch needles have a very sharp point and can be used with two threads going through the needle's eye; the eyes on topstitch needles are larger than on universal needles. They help to create defined stitches for a neat, even finish.

Microtex needles are another great option for bag making, as they are ideal for topstitching and ensuring accurate stitch lines. The tip on a microtex needle is a very sharp and precise point, meaning that on thick woven fabric you can maintain a straight topstitch line that you may not be able to achieve with a universal needle.

MACHINE FEET

There are two main machine feet that I recommend for bag making. The first is a walking foot. This is a foot that has feed dogs on the underside that move with the needle falling and rising. This means that both the top and the bottom of the sewing machine are 'walking' the fabric through the machine at the same speed, ensuring that the layers stay together as they should and there are no puckers in the stitching. It can also help with sewing over thick seams and bulky fabrics. You can use the walking foot for most sewing on a bag and so it doesn't need to be removed. It does sound a little clunky, though, so be prepared for that.

The second foot that you will need is an adjustable piping/zipper foot. This is a narrow foot that can be adjusted for the edge of the foot to be placed wherever you would like it to in relation to the needle. You can get a perfectly straight line of topstitching next to a zip with the adjustable foot by lowering your needle, placing the foot on the machine and then aligning the edge of the foot with where the needle enters the fabric. You don't need to worry about a bulky heel on a regular zipper foot, which makes inserting zips a real pleasure.

Walking foot

Adjustable piping/zipper foot

THREADS

For a really strong finish, consider using a good-quality polyester thread for bag making. Polyester tends to shred less and is often slightly waxy, resulting in a neater finish through thick layers. It's better on handles and straps than cotton thread, which can perish over time, especially if anything of weight is added to the bag. On an overnight bag, for example, you want to be sure that you can trust the thread to carry the weight of your belongings!

The lower the number assigned to a thread, the thicker it is. For a really neat defined topstitch, try using a 'topstitch thread', which is designed to create defined stitches and looks great when sewn in a contrast colour. However, you should steer clear of contrast thread colours unless you can be confident of sewing a straight seam: a well-matched thread a shade darker than the fabric will always be less noticeable if you tend towards a little wobble as you sew.

BAG BASES

For a rigid bag base, choose a plastic grid canvas or mesh. This can easily stand the rigours of a well-used bag and prevents a bag from 'sagging' under the weight of any personal possessions.

For a budget-friendly option, try thin flexible cutting mats cut to size. Foam core board is an excellent option for bags such as an overnight bag that will carry a lot of weight. It is made up of two sheets of thick cardboard with lightweight foam sandwiched between. While it is lightweight and easy to cut to size, it maintains its structure in a bag where weight will be evenly distributed, preventing the bag base from sagging under pressure. You can buy it in an art supply shop as it's usually used for mounting artworks.

ZIPS

In bag making, the sizes of zip that are most commonly used are #3 and #5. These numbers refer to the width of the zip teeth. A #3 has 3mm (⅛in) wide teeth and a #5 has 5mm (¼in) wide teeth.

In lining pockets and smaller pouches, a #3 zip is ideal; sew 6mm (¼in) from the edge of the zip tape. Bags with a zip closure tend to use a #5 zip and these are sewn 1cm (⅜in) from the edge of the zip tape.

The length of a zip is measured from the start to the end of the teeth: 15, 18 and 20cm (6, 7 and 8in) zips are great lengths for lining zip pockets, while 25, 30 and 35cm (10, 12 and 14in) zips are good lengths for bag closures.

A continuous zip is zip tape that comes on a roll and is sold by the metre (yard); you add the zip pulls to it and cut it to size as needed.

NOTE

If you'd like to use continuous zips, cut the finished zip at least 5cm (2in) longer than the pattern calls for to allow space to attach it.

Continuous zip

#3 zip

Bag bases

#5 zip

Techniques

Here are a few essential techniques that you will use time and time again for all your bag making projects.

PATTERN PIECES

All of the shaped pattern pieces for the projects in this book are provided. Measurements are given for any rectangular pieces, although you may prefer to draw them out on paper. Measurements are given in both metric and imperial; to ensure accuracy, follow one system or the other throughout – but don't mix the two.

Where there is a 'fold' arrow on a pattern piece, fold the fabric and line up the 'fold' arrow edge with this fold. Pin the pattern piece in place and cut around it to create your full-width panel.

Sometimes, the same pattern piece is used to cut more than one piece; this will be indicated on the pattern piece by a dotted line. In these instances, cut the pattern to the largest size and then fold it on the dotted line and treat that as the outer line to cut out the other panel.

CUTTING OUT

Give the paper patterns a dry press with an iron to remove any creases. Using paper scissors, cut around each pattern piece. Pin the pattern piece to the fabric, or use pattern weights if you're using a rotary cutter, and cut out.

SEAM ALLOWANCES

Seam allowances are all included in the projects in this book. The majority are 1cm (⅜in), but double check on each project page before sewing. This is a great seam allowance for bags: it's not so wide that it creates a lot of extra bulk, but it's not so narrow that you need to worry about a bag coming apart during use.

BLOCK FUSING

If you will be using a lot of interfaced fabric, you may wish to fuse the interfacing to the wrong side of the fabric before you cut out any panels. This will save time as you're only cutting once, but you can end up wasting fabric as, once it's been interfaced, you may not be able to use it for anything else. To be thrifty, you can cut out all of the pieces from interfacing first and then carefully arrange them on your fabric to reduce fabric wastage. Fuse the interfacing pieces in place, then cut around them.

TOPSTITCHING

Topstitching is usually done 3mm (⅛in) from the seam or edge. This gives a nice neat finish and holds things in place. Sometimes topstitching is purely decorative, to give a professional look; sometimes it's for a practical reason – for example, to keep linings down inside the bag or prevent fabric from getting caught in a zip.

Pockets

In this section you'll learn how to create pockets, from the simplest slip pocket to more complex zipped dividers. Using the techniques shown here, you can add pockets to any bag pattern you wish, customizing your bag to suit your own needs. Don't forget that you can layer pockets on top of one another: as long as they're each joined securely to the lining panel, you can create any configuration you choose!

2

Top tip 1

Reinforce the stitching at both top edges by backstitching: it's an awful hassle to reinforce after your bag is completed!

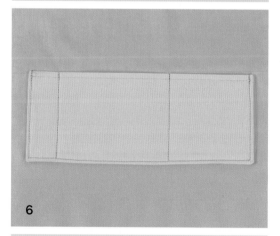

6

Top tip 2

Make sure you stitch directly on top of the previous stitching for a super-neat finish.

SLIP POCKETS

SIMPLE SLIP POCKET

A simple slip pocket is a great addition to any bag. You can customize it to fit the bag perfectly, holding whatever you need.

For a simple slip pocket, lay out the main panel for the bag you are making to determine what size and shape to cut. It's best not to have a slip pocket too close to the top or the base of the bag, so aim for the finished pocket to end at least 2.5cm (1in) from the base and 5cm (2in) from the top – except in clutch bags, where everything is near the base!

If you're making a bag with boxed corners or darts, measure the width of the lining panel inside the finished corners. As for height, around about 15cm (6in) is the deepest pocket that is practical. Consider what the pocket will be used for and adjust as necessary. For example, if you're going to be carrying a book in the pocket, you'll want to make the pocket deeper than usual.

If you prefer to use paper pattern pieces, draw the pocket on scrap paper before you cut. Don't forget to add the seam allowance! For bag making, 1cm (⅜in) is a perfect seam allowance; if you'd like to use this, then cut the pocket to your desired final width + 2cm (¾in). For the height, make life easy for yourself and cut the pocket to twice the desired final height + 2cm (¾in).

1 Once you've decided on the final size of your pocket, cut one piece of pocket fabric and one piece of medium-weight interfacing, then fuse the interfacing to the wrong side of the pocket fabric (*see Tools & Materials: Interfacing and Stabilizers*). Don't forget to add interfacing to the lining panel before you attach any pockets.

2 Fold the pocket panel in half, right sides together, then sew around the three open edges, leaving a turning gap in one edge (*see Professional Touches: Turning Gaps*).

3 Clip the corners (*see Professional Touches: Dealing with Bulk*), turn the pocket right side out and push out the corners. Turn under the turning gap seam allowance and press well. Topstitch along the folded edge, 3mm (⅛in) from the edge.

4 Place the pocket on the lining panel at whichever distance you determined when making your template, then topstitch it in place around the sides and bottom, again stitching 3mm (⅛in) from the edge. This will also close the turning gap. *See Top Tip 1.*

DIVIDED SLIP POCKET

To make a divided slip pocket, follow steps 1–4 of the Simple Slip Pocket. Once you're ready to sew it to the lining, add some extra topstitching to make this practical pocket even more useful.

5 Using a chalk marker and a ruler, mark lines on the slip pocket to determine where the divisions will be sewn. As a rough guide, 2.5cm (1in) from the edge forms a great pen slot, while 11.5cm (4½in) is ideal for most smart phones or a pack of pocket tissues.

6 Start with the needle at one top corner edge of the slip pocket, backstitch to reinforce the start, and then sew down the side. Continue along the bottom to the first division line. With the needle still in the fabric, lift the presser foot and pivot the fabric through 90 degrees. Sew up the division line to the top, backstitch a couple of stitches, then return to the top. With the needle still in the fabric, lift the presser foot and pivot 180 degrees. Sew back down the line to the bottom, pivot 90 degrees and continue. Repeat this as many times as is needed to divide the pocket fully. *See Top Tip 2.*

REINFORCED SLIP POCKET

7 If you're concerned that the weight of the contents will put undue stress on the pocket, it's easy to add reinforcements to the top corners. Simply insert a rivet into each top corner (*see Hardware & Bling: Rivets*). You'll need to add some bulk behind the main panel to secure the post, so cut some scraps of foam stabilizer approximately 1.5cm (⅝in) square and pop them onto the rivet post on the wrong side of the main panel before adding the cap. You shouldn't need more than two per rivet.

FULL-WIDTH SLIP POCKET

A full-width slip pocket is one that is sewn into the side and bottom edges of the bag, with only the top seam visible. This could be for a laptop, folder, book, travel card or even an easy-access phone. It's great for creating extra pockets without adding too much extra bulk for designs where sleek lines are needed.

8 To cut the pattern piece for a full-width slip pocket, you'll need to use the main body pattern piece. Decide how far down you would like the pocket to start, then fold the pattern piece at that measurement. As long as you use the same seam allowance as for sewing the main bag these will cancel each other out, so you can disregard adding or removing seam allowances. For example, if you'd like the pocket to start 5cm (2in) from the top of the main panel, simply fold the main body panel 5cm (2in) from the top, then treat the folded pattern piece edge as the top edge.

9 Once you've decided on the final size of the pocket, cut two pieces of pocket fabric and two pieces of medium-weight interfacing, then fuse the interfacing to the wrong side of the pocket fabric (*see Tools & Materials: Interfacing and Stabilizers*). Don't forget to add interfacing to the main panel before you attach any pockets.

10 If you'd like to add a magnetic snap to the full-width slip pocket, attach the male half of the snap in the centre of one pocket panel, on the right side of the fabric, with the edge of the washer 2.5cm (1in) from the top edge (*see Hardware & Bling: Magnetic Snaps*). Sew both pocket panels right sides together along the top edge, then fold them wrong sides together and press well.

11 Topstitch the top edge, stitching 3mm (⅛in) from the edge. For a very large pocket, you may wish to add a second row of topstitching 3mm (⅛in) from the first (*see Core Skills: Topstitching*).

12 To position the second half of the magnetic snap, match up the bottom and side edges of the full-width pocket and the main panel, then press the snap hard onto the main panel. Lift up the pocket and you should see an indentation, which you can mark to denote the centre of the female half of the snap. Insert the female half of the magnetic snap and then tack (baste) the pocket to the main panel, matching the raw edges.

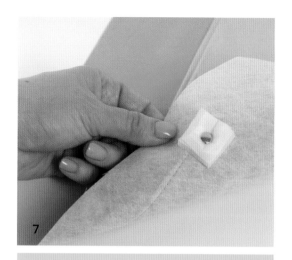

7

Top tip

Add full-width pockets to the back of bags for easy access to valuables such as phones and e-readers.

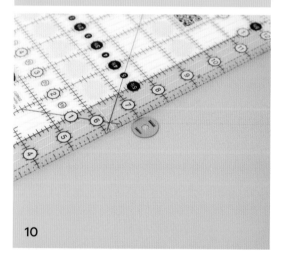

10

Top tip

Pockets aren't just for linings: you can easily customize a bag to your own requirements by adding pockets to the exterior, under a flap or even inside other pockets!

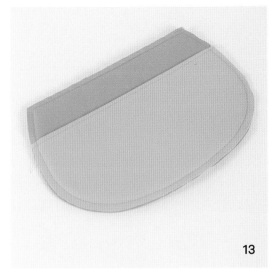

13

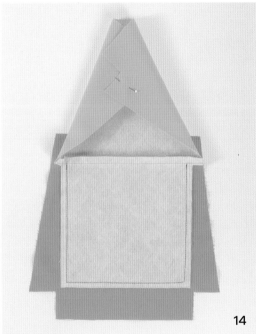

14

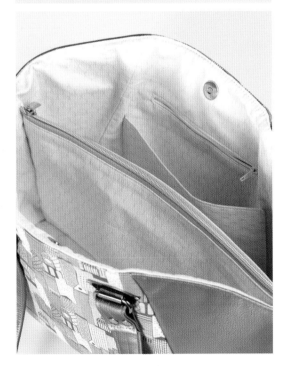

13 For a bag with a rounded shape with darts or a gusset, lay the full-width pocket in place on the main panel, matching the raw edges, and tack (baste) around all edges within the seam allowance.

14 For a bag with boxed corners, lay the full-width pocket in place on the main panel, matching the raw edges, then lift up the top layer of the pocket. Pin the bottom layer in place, then mark a line 1.2cm (½in) from each edge of the boxed corners. Stitching only the pocket layer to the main panel layer, sew down one line, along the bottom line and back up the other, then only trim the pocket panel fabric from this seam. This will reduce bulk in the boxed corners and ensure that items don't get lost in the base.

TECH POCKET

To add a pocket specifically for tech such as an e-reader or a tablet, choose whether a simple slip pocket or a full-width slip pocket is more appropriate for the size of the device vs the size of the main panel. Add foam stabilizer to the inner pocket piece (*see Tools & Materials: Interfacing and Stabilizers*), then treat as described above for the type of pocket you've chosen. The foam stabilizer will add extra protection to the screen of the device in the pocket.

A magnetic snap may not be the best option for a tech pocket; substitute hook-and-loop tape to prevent scratches.

ALL-IN-ONE CARD HOLDER, SLIP AND LIPBALM POCKET

FINISHED POCKET SIZE (W x H)

22 x 9.5cm (8⅝ x 3¾in)

CUTTING INSTRUCTIONS

To make this configuration, cut the following. The sizes given below are width x height and include a 6mm (¼in) seam allowance. You will need two different-coloured fabric markers, a Hera marker and a steam iron.

From lining fabric:

- For A (Card Holder), cut one piece 11.5 x 37cm (4½ x 14¾in)

- For B (Slip and Lipbalm Pockets), cut one piece 18 x 10.5cm (7 x 4¼in)

- For C (Pocket Backing), cut one piece 28 x 10.5cm (11 x 4¼in)

From medium-weight interfacing:

- For A (Card Holder), cut three pieces 9.5 x 1.2cm (3¾ x ½in)

- For B (Slip and Lipbalm Pockets), cut one piece 18 x 10.5cm (7 x 4¼in)

15 Fuse the medium-weight interfacing to both the slip and lipbalm pockets (B).

16 On the wrong side of the card holder piece (A), write TOP on the top edge and then draw a series of horizontal lines at the distances shown in the photo. You may wish to use different colours to differentiate them. You will be pressing the fabric along these lines, so a heat-erasable pen is not recommended. The blue lines will be folded right sides together; the pink lines will be folded wrong sides together.

17 Fuse a piece of card holder interfacing (A) slightly underneath each pink line and centred on the width of the panel.

18 Score the first line with a Hera marker and then flip the panel over so that it's right side up. Fold the panel right sides together (RST) along the scored line and press.

19 Flip the panel over so that it's wrong side up, then score the next line with the Hera marker. Fold the panel wrong sides together (WST) along the scored line and press. There should be 1.2cm (½in) between the two blue lines.

16 (Wrong side of fabric)

17 (Wrong side of fabric)

Top tip

If you're struggling to work out which way up to have the card slots, ignore the photos and just follow the directions.

18 (Right side of fabric)

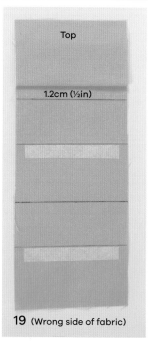

19 (Wrong side of fabric)

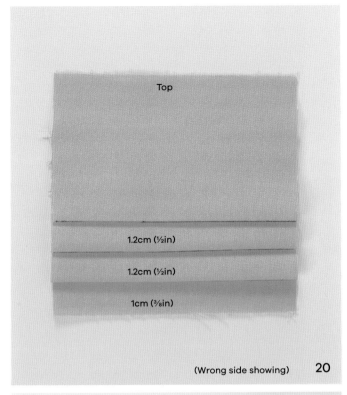

Top

1.2cm (½in)

1.2cm (½in)

1cm (⅜in)

(Wrong side showing) 20

21

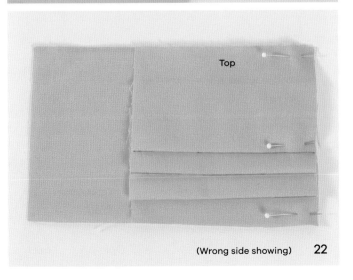

Top

(Wrong side showing) 22

20 Repeat for the remaining lines, alternating between folding RST and WST. On the wrong side there should be 1.2cm (½in) between lines, and the distance from the last fold to the edge of the panel should be 1cm (⅜in).

21 Working on the right side, topstitch along the three folds with interfacing attached, stitching 3mm (⅛in) from the folds, then re-fold.

22 With right sides together, matching the raw edges on the right, place the folded card holder panel (A) on top of the slip and lipbalm pockets (B). Sew together using the regular 6mm (¼in) seam allowance, then open and press the seam allowances away from the card holder panel.

23 Place the pocket backing (C) on top, right sides together, and sew around all four edges, leaving a turning gap on one side (*see Professional Touches: Turning Gaps*).

24 Clip the corners and turn the pocket through. Turn under the turning gap seam allowance and press well, then topstitch along the top edge, stitching 3mm (⅛in) from the edge.

25 The finished pocket panel will be 22cm (8⅝in) wide, which is wider than the finished pocket size at this stage. Using a chalk pen, mark where each edge should finish on the main panel, then lay the pocket on top. Pin the left-hand edge of the slip pocket to the main panel, aligning it with your chalk mark, then make a mark 10.5cm (4¼in) from this edge. This will be the start of the lipbalm section; pin the inner corners of the slip pocket at this mark. Align the right-hand edge of the card holder with the right-hand chalk mark on the main panel, and pin the outer corners in place.

26 Starting at the top right-hand edge, topstitch the pocket panel In place, 3mm (⅛in) from the edge. Sew from the top, pivot at the corner, and sew along the bottom until you get to the first seam. Pivot and sew up the seam 'in the ditch' to the top edge and backstitch. Trim the thread, then start again at the top left-hand edge, sew from the top, pivot at the corner and continue sewing until you're 10.5cm (4¼in) from the left-hand edge. Pivot and sew to the top edge, backstitch and trim the thread.

27 Flatten the lipbalm pocket to form a box pleat, pin, then sew across the bottom edge to secure it in place.

ELASTICATED POCKET FOR A PANEL

Elasticated pockets are great for holding bulkier items such as changes of clothes in a baby bag, trainers in a gym bag or yarn in a crafting bag. You'll need 1cm (⅜in) wide elastic and a safety pin or bodkin.

28 To create a pattern piece for an elasticated pocket you'll need to decide how wide and how high you'd like the finished pocket to be, based on the size of the main panel. Don't forget to add interfacing to the lining panel before you attach any pockets. On a piece of paper, draw a vertical line near the left-hand edge that's the height you'd like the finished pocket plus twice the seam allowance. For example, for a pocket that's 15cm (6in) high, draw a line that is 15cm + 1cm + 1cm (6in + ⅜in + ⅜in). From the bottom of this line, draw a horizontal line the total width you'd like the pocket bottom to be plus twice the seam allowance.

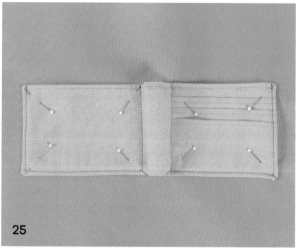

25

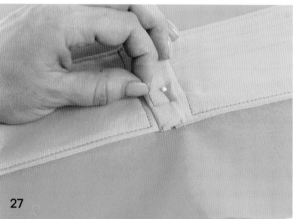

27

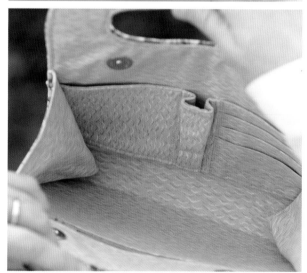

Top tip

This handy pocket can be added anywhere you choose. It'll fit standard credit cards and lipbalms, so is ideal for clutch bags and work bags alike.

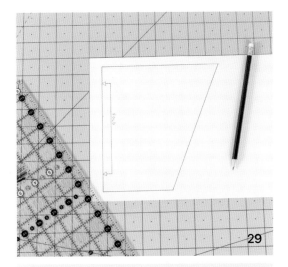

29

29 From the top of the vertical line, draw a horizontal line to the total width of the fabric to cut. As a rule of thumb, making this line 60% longer than the bottom edge will give the pocket a practical depth. To calculate the length of the top line, multiply the length of the bottom line by 1.6. For example, the bottom line is 10cm (4in); multiplying this by 1.6 gives 16cm (6½in) = 18cm (7¼in). Draw a fold arrow on the left-hand vertical line, then connect the top and bottom lines on the right. You now have the pattern piece for your custom elasticated pocket!

30 Once you've cut this paper pattern piece out, cut two pieces on the fold from lining fabric and one on the fold from medium-weight interfacing. Fuse the interfacing to the wrong side of one lining panel.

31 Add two marks either side within the seam allowance at 1.2cm (½in) and 2.5cm (1in) from the top. Pin the two lining fabric panels right sides together and sew around all four sides, stopping and starting at the two marks either side to leave a 1.2cm (½in) gap and leaving a turning gap along the bottom edge (*see Professional Touches: Turning Gaps*).

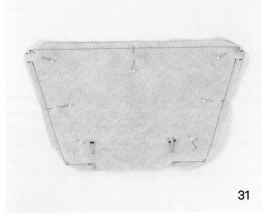

31

32 Clip the corners and turn the pocket right side out, pushing all seams out well (*see Professional Touches: Neat Corners*). Press well.

33 Topstitch across the top edge of the pocket, 3mm (⅛in) from the top edge and 1.2cm (½in) below this to form a casing for the elastic.

34 Cut a piece of elastic the width of the bottom of the pocket. For the example here, this will be 20cm (8in) as the panel was cut on the fold. Attach a safety pin or bodkin to the end of the elastic, thread it through the casing until the end of the elastic is near the opening, then secure with a few rows of stitching.

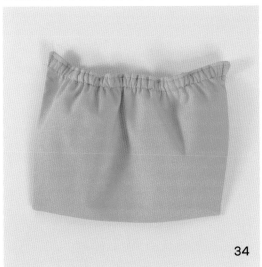

34

35 Position the elasticated pocket on the main panel, making sure the bottom edge is straight and centred, then pin it in place. Straighten the pocket sides so that the bottom corners are square. Topstitch along the side and bottom edges, stitching 3mm (⅛in) from the edge and catching the turning gap in the stitching. You may need to manipulate the panel as you feed it through the sewing machine to ensure that it stays flat.

36 To divide the pocket, flatten it as best you can, then pin it in place to enable you to mark and sew the dividing lines.

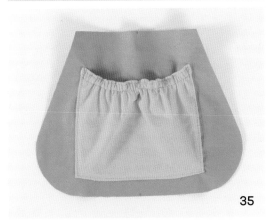

35

ELASTICATED POCKET SEWN INTO SIDE SEAMS

This easy-to-sew elasticated pocket is sewn into both side edges of the bag, meaning that the pocket sides can be left raw – great for smaller bags or bags with side gussets!

37 To create the pattern piece for the pocket, measure the width of the panel the pocket is to be sewn onto; this will form the bottom edge measurement. Add 60% by multiplying by 1.6; this will form the top edge measurement. Draw two lines to these lengths, centring the bottom edge on the top edge, with the distance between them being the desired height of the finished pocket + twice the seam allowance, then join the two sides to create a tumbler shape.

38 Using the paper pattern piece, cut two panels from lining fabric and one panel from medium-weight interfacing. Fuse the interfacing to the wrong side of one main panel. Sew the panels right sides together along the top and bottom edges only.

39 Turn the pocket right side out and press, making sure the seams are pushed out fully. Topstitch across the top edge of the pocket 3mm (⅛in) from the top edge and 1.2cm (½in) below this to form a casing for the elastic.

40 Cut the elastic to the same length as the bottom of the tumbler. Attach a safety pin or bodkin to the end of the elastic and thread it through the casing until 6mm (¼in) of elastic is sticking out of each end, then secure at both ends with tacking (basting) stitches.

41 Position the pocket on the main body panel and tack (baste) in place along the sides within the seam allowance. Topstitch the bottom in place 3mm (⅛in) from the edge.

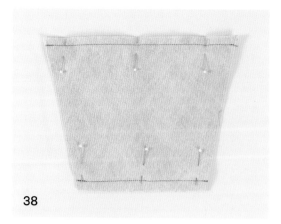

38

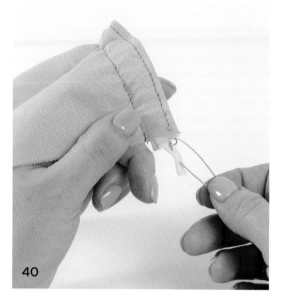

40

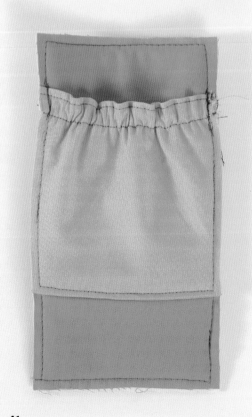

41

Top tip

An adjustable zip foot is a really handy tool for sewing super-neat zips *(see Tools & Materials: Machine Feet).*

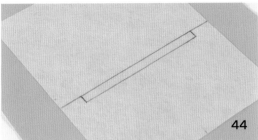
44

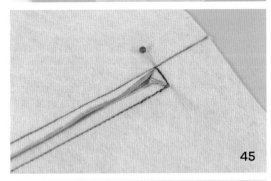
45

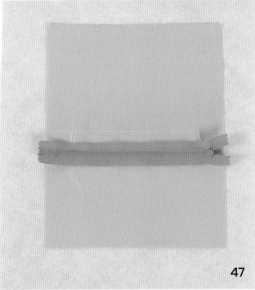
47

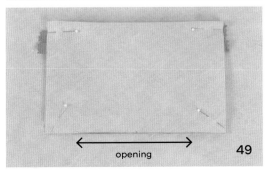

← opening →
49

ZIP POCKETS

SIMPLE ZIP POCKET

This zip pocket is the quickest and simplest to install. It's a classic method and results in a great practical pocket. You'll need a #3 zip the length of the zip opening *(see Tools & Materials: Zips).*

42 First, measure which size pocket the main panel can comfortably accommodate. Cut the pocket to this width, but twice the height; cut one lining piece and one interfacing piece, then fuse the interfacing to the wrong side of the lining.

43 To create the zip box opening, fold the panel in half heightwise, right sides together, and draw a horizontal line across the panel 1.2cm (½in) below the fold. Intersect this line 2.5cm (1in) from each side edge, then finish creating the rectangle by drawing a line 1cm (⅜in) below the first horizontal line. The box will be 1cm (⅜in) high and the width of the pocket minus 5cm (2in) in width.

44 Place the pocket panel on top of the main panel, right sides together. The bottom of the zip pocket panel should be at least 1.2cm (½in) from the bottom of the lining panel. Pin it in place, then sew around the outside of the marked zip box. Stop with the needle down at each corner, lift the presser foot and pivot before lowering the presser foot and continuing to sew. Draw a line through the centre of the box lengthwise and then mark a 1.2cm (½in) triangle at each end.

45 Steam press the stitches, then pull the zip pocket up and away from the main panel, steam pressing all edges. Insert a pin through each short end of the box on the stitch line. Using a seam ripper or small scissors, cut along the centre line and through each small triangle to the corners of the box. The pins will ensure that you don't snip the box stitches in the trimming process. Clip as close to them as possible.

46 Remove the pins, then push the zip pocket through to the wrong side of the main panel and press well from the main panel side. This will mean that any small creases are hidden on the inside of the pocket, resulting in a really neat finish.

47 Add some double-sided basting tape to the inside of the pocket side above and below the box as close to the edge as possible, then place the zip right side down. It's up to you which end the zip pull is; it's most commonly placed to the left on a lining panel, but there's no right or wrong direction for this.

48 Stitch around all four edges of the outside of the box as close as is comfortable – at most, 3mm (⅛in) from the edge of the box. This will secure the zip in place. Match the bobbin thread to the zip colour, as the stitches will be seen on the inside.

49 Finally, on the wrong side of the lining panel bring the top of the zip pocket down to meet the bottom raw edge and sew around the three open edges.

NOTE

If you want to turn the bag through the pocket to hide the turning gap, remember to leave a turning gap large enough to fit the whole bag through at the bottom of the zip pocket. If you've done this, remember to open the zip and leave it open!

HIDDEN TAPE ZIP POCKET

Take your zip pockets to a new professional level with this updated pocket technique in which the zip tapes are hidden within the pocket seams. You'll need a #3 zip 5cm (2in) shorter than the width of the pocket panels (*see Tools & Materials: Zips*). Cut continuous zips to the width of the pocket panels.

50 First, measure which size pocket the main panel can comfortably accommodate. Cut the pocket to this width, and to the heights given in the cutting instructions; cut one lining piece and one interfacing piece, then fuse the interfacing to the lining.

CUTTING INSTRUCTIONS

From lining fabric:

- For A (Zip Pocket Facing), cut one piece [width of pocket] x 3.5cm (1⅜in) high

- For B (Zip Pocket Top), cut one piece [width of pocket] x [height of pocket] + 2.5cm (1in)

- For C (Zip Pocket Bottom), cut one piece [width of pocket] x [height of pocket]

From medium-weight interfacing:

- For A (Zip Pocket Facing), cut one piece [width of pocket] x 3.5cm (1⅜in) high

- For B (Zip Pocket Top), cut one piece [width of pocket] x [height of pocket] + 2.5cm (1in)

- For C (Zip Pocket Bottom), cut one piece [width of pocket] x [height of pocket]

51 On the right side of the fabric, apply a line of double-sided basting tape to the top edge of the zip pocket bottom (C). Place the #3 zip right side up on top, lining up the raw edges and centres, with the pull to the right. Stitch in place along the top edge of the zip only, stitching 6mm (¼in) from the edge.

52 Fold the zip over to the wrong side and press it in place. Do not topstitch at this point.

53 On the right side of the fabric, apply a line of double-sided basting tape to the top edge of the zip pocket top (B), then turn the piece so that the top edge is at the bottom. This is particularly important for directional fabrics. With the zip pocket top (B) right side up and the zip pocket bottom (C) right side down, match then sew the other edge of the zip to the upper raw edge of the zip pocket top (B), using a scant 6mm (¼in) seam allowance. The zip should be right side up, with the zip pull to the right.

54 Press both fabrics away from the zip so that the zip lies flat, with the right side of the zip showing on the wrong side of the fabrics and the zip pull to the left. The larger panel is the zip pocket top (B).

Zip right side up

Zip pocket bottom, right side up

52

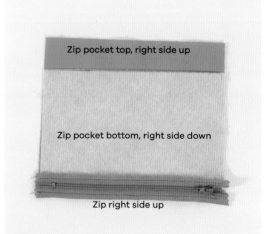

Zip pocket top, right side up

Zip pocket bottom, right side down

Zip right side up

53

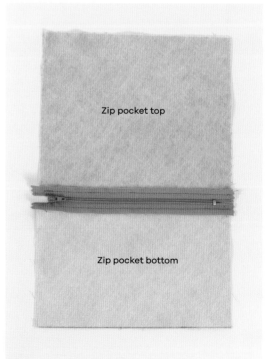

Zip pocket top

Zip pocket bottom

54

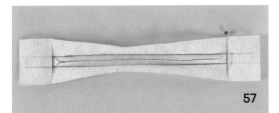

57

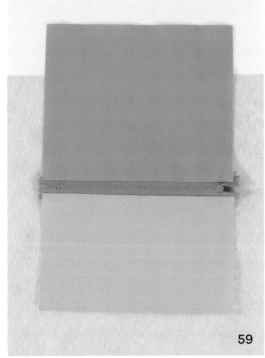

59

55 On the wrong side of the zip pocket facing (A), draw a box that is 1.2cm (½in) from each long edge and 2.5cm (1in) from each short edge. The resulting box will be 1cm (⅜in) high and the length of the zip teeth. Place the zip pocket facing (A) on top of the main panel, right sides together, with the edge of the facing at least 2.5cm (1in) from the top of the main panel. Wherever the box is placed is where the zip opening will be on the main panel.

56 Pin the zip pocket facing (A) in place, then sew around the outside of the box. Stop with the needle down at each corner, lift the presser foot and pivot before lowering the presser foot and continuing to sew. Once the box is fully sewn, steam press the stitches, then pull the zip pocket facing up and away from the lining panel, steam pressing all edges.

57 Draw a line through the centre of the box lengthwise and then a small 1.2cm (½in) triangle at each end. Insert a pin through each short end of the box on the stitch line. Using a seam ripper or small scissors, cut along the centre line and through each small triangle to the corners of the box. The pins will ensure that you don't snip the box stitches in the trimming process. Clip as close to them as possible.

58 Remove the pins, then push the zip pocket facing (A) through to the wrong side of the lining and press well from the lining side. This will mean that any small creases are hidden on the inside of the pocket resulting in a really neat finish.

59 Apply a line of double-sided basting tape to the top and bottom of the zip pocket facing (A) box on the right side. Place the zip panel right side up on top of the basting tape on the zip pocket facing, aligning the zip evenly and ensuring that the zip pull is showing in the gap.

The lining panel should be right side down. Once the position is correct, press down well to adhere the zip panel to the tape. Turn the panel over to ensure that the zip can be seen through the gap.

60 With the zip pocket top and bottom flat, stitch around all four edges of the outside of the box opening 3mm (⅛in) from the edge to secure the zip to the panel.

61 Finally, on the wrong side of the lining panel, bring the top of the zip pocket down to meet the bottom raw edge and sew around the three open edges.

Top tip

If you want to turn the bag through the pocket to hide the turning gap, remember to leave a turning gap large enough to fit the whole bag through at the bottom of the zip pocket. If you've done this, remember to open the zip and leave it open!

ZIPPED DIVIDERS

Take your bag making to a whole new level with a professional-finish zipped divider. This method works for bags with boxed corners and has a clever way of achieving this almost freestanding zip pocket.

NOTE

This divider is easiest if you trim away the fabric from the boxed corners on the lining main panels before starting (*see Shaping: Cut-out Boxed Corners*).

62 To calculate the size of the zipped divider pieces, measure the bottom edge of the lining panel inside the corner cut-outs. Next measure the side edge of the lining panel at 90 degrees to the bottom edge above the corner cut-out to decide how high to make the divider. Don't place this too near the top open edge of the bag; remember to leave space for your closure hardware. Cut four pieces of divider fabric and four pieces of medium-weight interfacing. You will also need a #3 or #5 zip the same length as the width of the divider fabric (*see Tools & Materials: Zips*).

63 Fuse the interfacing to the wrong side of the divider fabric pieces. Place a line of double-sided basting tape along the top edge of a divider panel, on the right side. Place the zip right side down on the tape, matching the raw edges, then place another divider panel right side down on top, matching the raw edges. Stitch along the top edge through all three layers, 6mm (¼in) from the edge, then fold the wrong sides together and press, pulling the fabric away from the zip teeth. Topstitch 3mm (⅛in) from the edge. Repeat to attach the remaining divider panels to the second side of the zip.

64 Pull the panels of the zipped divider flat so they are right sides together, with the zip sandwiched in the centre.

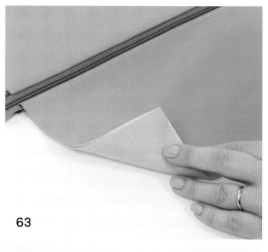

63

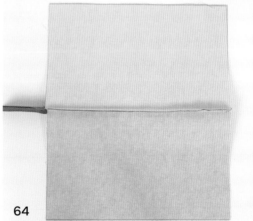

64

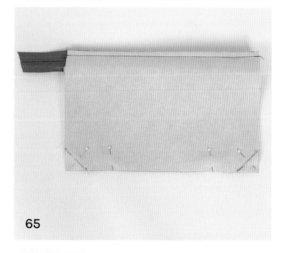

65

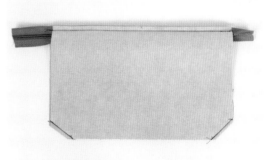

66

67

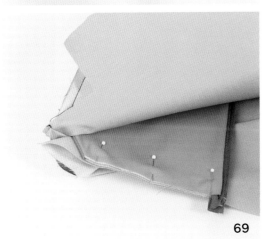

69

70

65 Pull the top panel stack down to match the raw edges of the bottom panel stack. All four layers will now be together in one stack. Make a mark 3cm (1¼in) from each bottom corner on the sides and bottom of the stack, then connect with a line to form a triangle in each corner.

66 Sew along the triangle lines through all four layers, trim the seam allowances, turn right side out and press, ensuring that the corner cut-outs are pushed out fully. The side and bottom edges will be raw. You may wish to remove the zip teeth 1.2cm (½in) from each edge to reduce bulk when sewing into the side seams.

67 Lay the zipped divider right side up on one lining panel, matching the centres and bottom edges.

68 Lay the second lining panel right side down on top, matching the raw edges. Stitch along the bottom edge only, through all layers.

69 Pull the top lining panel back out of the way, then match the zipped divider to the side of the lining, placing it 3cm (1¼in) from the top of the corner cut-out. Pin to hold.

70 Bring the second lining panel over, matching the side raw edges, and pin all the layers together. The lining will have to fold in order to match the side edges. Repeat for the second side edge. To finish sewing the lining, stitch from the bottom of the lining panel to the top on both sides through all layers. You can then continue to sew the boxed corners (*see Shaping: Cut-out Boxed Corners*).

Top tip

A zipped divider is great for keeping bags organized and keeping important items safely zipped away.

Zip Closures

In this section, you'll master zip closures and learn how to add a zip to any bag pattern, altering it to suit your own personal needs. You'll need an adjustable piping/zipper foot and double-sided basting tape for great zip closures. For more information on these, as well as sizes and types of zip to use, *see Tools & Materials*.

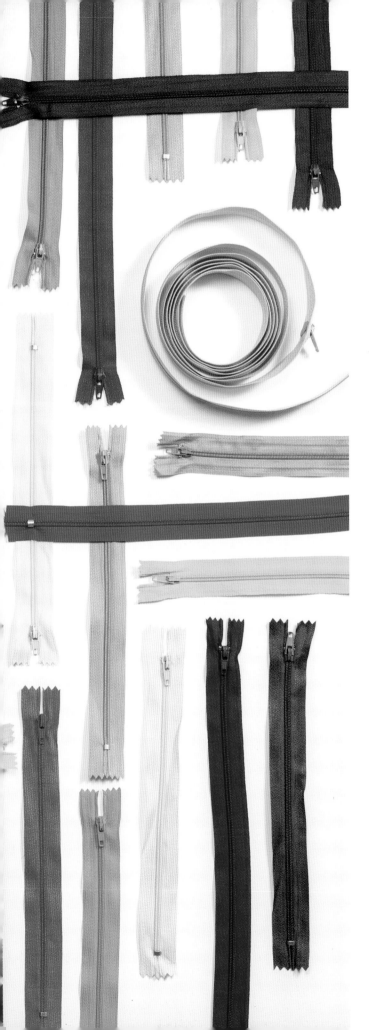

ZIP BRIDGES

A zip bridge is a zip that spans the opening at the top of a bag, usually sitting down inside the bag so that it is only visible when you're looking at the bag from above. There are two methods for creating one. Both are great for creating a secure finish to a bag with a simple shape, such as a darted base, a boxed-corner base and a bag with a bottom gusset only.

Start by measuring the top of the finished bag, then choose a zip that is slightly longer. I like my zips to be around 5–7.5cm (2–3in) longer.

To cut the fabric and interfacing pieces, you will need the following measurements:

A – the finished width of the bag

B – half the finished depth of the bag

SPLITTING A LINING

This is when the zip bridge is going to be inserted in the middle of a lining panel. You will need to alter the pattern piece of the lining main panel in order to divide it into two separate sections.

ALTERING THE PATTERN

1 Draw a line on the pattern piece for the lining main panel where you'd like the zip closure to sit, remembering to take into account the seam allowance at the top of the bag. Choose the seam allowance you'd like to use to attach the lining top to the lining bottom with the zip bridge in between; I usually choose 1cm (⅜in).

2 Draw the seam allowance below the line you've previously drawn. This will determine where the bottom of the upper section of the lining will be cut. Fold the pattern piece along this line and then cut the fabric and interfacing to this folded piece.

3 To make the pattern piece for the lower section of the lining, unfold the pattern piece, and draw the seam allowance above the first line that you drew. Fold and treat as before; this will give you two panels that, when sewn together with the zip bridge sandwiched in between, are the same size as the original lining main panel.

PREPARING THE ZIP BRIDGE AND ZIP

4 For the zip bridge, cut four pieces of fabric measuring A + 1cm (⅜in) long x (B/2) + 2cm (¾in) wide. Cut four pieces of interfacing to match, then fuse to each piece of fabric.

5 Fold both sides of the zip tape to the wrong side at right angles, matching the fold to the edge of the zip, then add some stitches to secure.

SEWING THE ZIP BRIDGE

6 Turn under 1cm (⅜in) on each short edge of all four zip bridge pieces and press in place.

7 With one zip bridge right side up, apply double-sided basting tape to one raw edge between the folded ends. Place the zip on top, right side down, matching the edge of the tape with the raw edge of the zip bridge. Add double-sided basting tape to the edge of the zip, then lay another zip bridge on top, right side down, matching the raw edges of the zip tape and zip bridge.

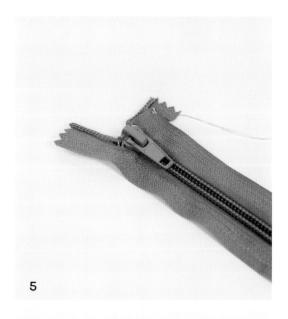

5

6

7

Top tip

If you are right-handed, you may wish to place the open end of the zip to the right of whichever lining panel you'd like on the back of the bag. If you are left-handed, you may wish to place the open end of the zip to the left of the back lining panel.

8 Unfold the short ends of the zip bridge, then stitch between the fold lines along the long raw edge.

9 Turn the zip bridge wrong sides together and press away from the zip. Fold the short open edges under along the fold line. Topstitch along each short edge and along the zip.

10 Repeat steps 7–9 with the remaining zip bridges and the second half of the zip. Leave approximately 1.2cm (½in) at the end of the zip after the metal stopper, then insert into a metal zip end (*see Hardware & Bling: Metal Zip End*) or sew a zip tab from a rectangle of faux leather approximately 3 x 7.5cm (1¼ x 3in).

11 Place one lower lining section panel right side up, then add the zip bridge on top, also right side up, lining up the raw edges.

12 Place the upper section of the lining panel right side down, again lining up the raw edges. Stitch through all four layers and press the seam towards the upper section of the lining panel. This will ensure that the zip bridge hangs down into the bag when it's open rather than sticking up. You may wish to topstitch on the lining upper at 3mm (⅛in) from the edge of the seam through all layers to keep everything in place.

13 Repeat steps 11 and 12 with the second set of upper and lower lining panels and the other half of the zip bridge. After sewing, open the zip fully and treat each half of the lining as an individual piece.

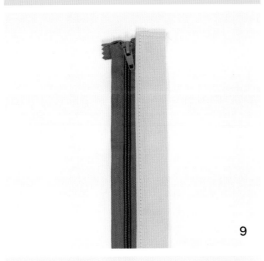

9

11

12

ADDING A ZIP BRIDGE ON TOP OF A LINING

This is where the zip bridge will be completely finished and then sewn onto the lining pieces with no alteration to the lining panels.

PREPARING THE FABRIC

14 To cut the fabric for the zip bridge for an unaltered lining, cut two pieces of fabric measuring A + 2cm (¾in) long x B + 2cm (¾in) high (*see Zip Bridges for A and B dimensions*). Cut two pieces of interfacing 1cm (⅜in) smaller all around, then fuse one to each piece of fabric.

SEWING THE ZIP BRIDGE

15 Turn under 1cm (⅜in) on all edges of both zip bridge pieces and press. You may wish to then open the folds and trim a little off each corner to help the zip bridge sit more neatly when finished.

16 Fold one zip bridge piece in half lengthways, wrong sides together, and press well to crease. Open the zip bridge and apply a line of double-sided basting tape along each pressed-under long edge. Place the raw edge on one side of the zip tape into the zip bridge on top of the basting tape, placing it with whichever seam allowance you feel most comfortable, then fold the second long edge of the zip bridge down and press it in place.

17 Topstitch along each short edge and along the zip, 3mm (⅛in) from the edge. Repeat with the remaining zip bridge and the second half of the zip.

18 Leave at least 1.2cm (½in) at the end of the zip tape after the metal stopper, then insert the end into a metal zip end (*see Hardware & Bling: Metal Zip End*) or sew a zip tab from a rectangle of faux leather approximately 3 x 7.5cm (1¼ x 3in).

19 Position the folded edge of the zip bridge however far down the lining panels you wish, making sure it's centred on the width. Topstitch along each folded edge of the zip bridge to secure it to the lining panels. After sewing, open the zip fully and treat each half of the lining as an individual piece.

16

17

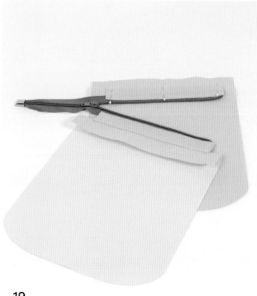

19

23

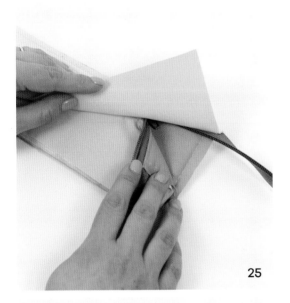

25

ZIP GUSSET CLOSURE

You can use this method for any bag with a gusset that continues all the way around the main panels, usually with a zip gusset on top attached to a base gusset that completes the circle. Most bags with a zip gusset call for bias binding on the inside seams, something that I can never seem to get neat; this method will replace the need for binding, leaving you time to enjoy your make!

PREPARING THE PANELS

20 Cut all of the pattern pieces for the bag as specified in the project and interface or stabilize them as detailed in the pattern. Separate out the exterior zip gussets, lining zip gussets, exterior base gusset and lining base gusset.

21 Follow the pattern instructions to prepare each main panel, both exterior and lining panels. Once each panel is complete, set them to one side and prepare the gusset.

22 For continuous zips, seal the ends to ensure that the zip pull doesn't get accidentally removed during sewing.

SEWING THE ZIP GUSSET

23 Apply a line of double-sided basting tape along one long edge of the right side of one exterior zip gusset. Place the zip right side down on top, matching the centres. Run another line of double-sided tape along the edge of the wrong side of the zip, then place one lining zip gusset right side down on top, matching the centres and raw edges.

24 Sew along the long edge. If you're using a #3 zip, stitch 6mm (¼in) from the edge of the tape; for a #5 zip, stitch 1cm (⅜in) from the edge. Turn the zip gussets wrong sides together and press well. Topstitch along the edge of the zip 3mm (⅛in) from the edge.

25 Repeat with the second side of the zip and the second exterior and lining zip gussets. Trim the zip gusset to the exact width of the base gusset. Do not trim the zip tails; this will prevent fraying during use. Make sure the zip pull is in the centre of the zip gusset.

26 Place the lining base gusset right side up, with the zip gusset panel right side down on top, matching the short edges. Pull back the exterior zip gusset, pin it out of the way and stitch the short ends of the lining base gusset together. You will need to do this in two sections, starting from the outside edge and stopping at the zip seam. Stitch as close to the zip seam as you can without going over it. Turn the panel over as needed to get access to sew.

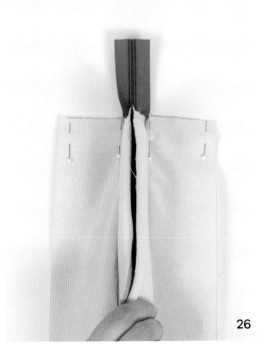

26

27 Repeat at the other end of the lining base gusset and the zip gusset.

28 If you're adding a strap tab to attach a long crossbody strap, now is the time to add them to the exterior base gusset panels.

29 Pull the lining panels back and repeat for the exterior base gusset and the exterior zip gusset. You should have the exterior base gusset sewn only to the exterior zip gusset and the lining base gusset sewn only to the lining zip gusset. Ensure that the zip is partially open so that the pull is not lost during the next step.

30 Turn the gussets wrong sides together and smooth the seam allowances down, away from the zip. Stitch across the top of the base gusset, for the width of the zip only, 3mm (⅛in) from the seam, through all layers, avoiding the metal stoppers, to close any holes.

31 If you would like to add a rivet, insert it 2cm (¾in) from the seam edge and centred on the width through all layers (*see Hardware & Bling: Rivets*).

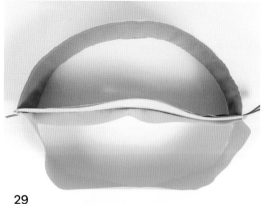

29

Top tip

Do not trim the excess zip tails; this will prevent fraying during use.

30

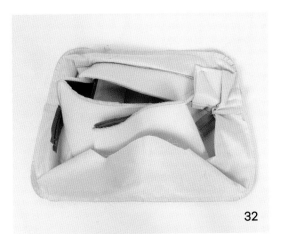

32

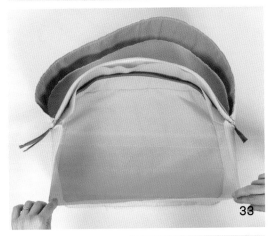

33

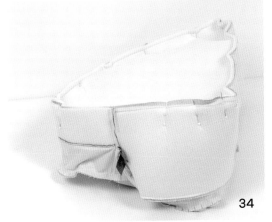

34

ATTACHING THE MAIN PANELS

If you haven't already marked the centres of the gussets and main panels, do so now.

32 Separate the lining zip gusset and base gusset from the exterior gussets and pin the lining main panel to one edge of the lining gusset, matching the centres. The easiest way to do this is to pin the centre and each bottom corner first, before working your way around. Try to ignore the exterior gussets while dealing with the lining pieces. For a tight-fitting gusset you may need to clip into the seam allowance to allow it to be sewn around the curves.

33 Stitch in place, with the gusset piece on top. Turn the bag so that the open edges of the gussets are open to you, and then repeat for the second lining main panel.

34 Turn the bag so that the exterior gusset is accessible and repeat for both exterior main panels. For particularly thick fabrics, try using a stapler to 'baste' the gusset to the main panels within the seam allowance. The staples will hold everything in place during sewing and can be trimmed off afterwards.

Top tip

Sewing with the gusset on top will always result in a neater finish; you're more able to control any puckers with the flat panel on the bottom and the gusset on top.

Hardware & Bling

Take your bags from amateur to professional by adding a little extra hardware and bling. It's so simple to do and it elevates a handmade bag from homemade to handcrafted. Mix and match, alter a pattern – the possibilities are endless.

You'll need a craft knife, a small hole punch, precision scissors, a small screwdriver set (magnetic is best), some Fray Check, scraps of interfacing and stabilizer, some duct tape and occasionally some strong glue. Shaped hole punches designed for leather work are also useful for cutting holes for twist locks and grommets.

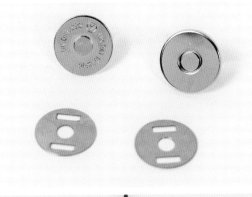

1

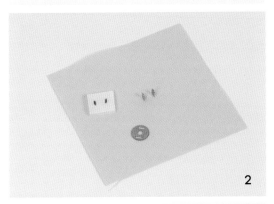

2

3

The completed snap

MAGNETIC SNAPS

REGULAR MAGNETIC SNAPS

Magnetic snaps are a staple in bag making. You can use them to secure flaps, close pockets and even to shape a wide bag gusset.

Each snap has a male part, a female part and two washers. There is no right or wrong way to place the snap, although the male part is commonly added to a flap or a pocket and the female part to the main part of a bag.

1 Use the cut-out lines in the washer to mark where you will make slits for the magnetic snap prongs.

2 Use a craft knife to slit through the marks, then add a dab of Fray Check to each slit. Push the prongs of the snap through the slits from the right side.

3 On the wrong side, add a scrap of stabilizer, followed by the washer, and then bend the prongs to secure. Place a small scrap of duct tape or interfacing over the top to prevent the prongs from rubbing through to the bag lining once constructed.

Top tip

It's slightly more secure to bend the prongs in on themselves; this will minimize the risk of the prongs slipping out of the slits over use.

DECORATIVE MAGNETIC SNAPS

You can use decorative magnetic snaps on any edge of a flap or pocket and they give a really polished finish to your bag.

Decorative magnetic snaps have a male part, a female part and any relevant fixings. The decorative part (usually the male part) is added to the exterior of the bag; the female part will be under the flap or inside the pocket, depending on where you are placing it.

If you can leave placing the female part until after you have constructed the bag and are able to reach through the turning gap to install it, you will end up with a more accurate placement. If you are applying the snap to a slip pocket, use the placement of the male part to determine where to position the female half.

4 Finish the pocket seam or the flap edge that you wish to add the decorative snap to and measure the thickness of the finished edge. If it is too thick to fit into the channel of the snap, give it a little hammer with a rubber mallet while protecting the fabric with some scrap fabric. This should help to compress it sufficiently to fit. If the fabric is too thin, slot it into the snap and then add a scrap of stabilizer, pushing it down inside with an awl.

5 Unscrew the centre screw holding the male part in place, add a dab of glue to the hole and then retighten the screw to secure. This will ensure that the screw does not work loose over use.

6 Add a dab of glue to any extra fixing screw holes and then add the screws. You may wish to pin a piece of scrap fabric over the finished decorative snap to minimize scratches as you finish constructing the bag.

7 Place the female half of the magnetic snap in the same way as for a regular magnetic snap.

LOCKS

TWIST LOCKS

These locks can add an extra layer of security to a bag or purse as well as being a great decorative feature. They're not difficult to fit, but you do need a little courage to cut through the finished bag to fit the female part.

Usually the female part has screws or prongs and the male part prongs. Any prongs should come with a washer for fitting.

8 Finish the flap or pocket that you'd like to add the female part to.

9 Use the washer to mark where to cut an opening and punch holes for the fixing screws.

10 Using precision scissors or a shaped hole punch, cut out the fabric around the outline of the female opening. Add holes for the screws. Apply Fray Check to the inside edges of all layers.

11 Place the female part right side down on a soft surface, with the flap right side down on top, aligning the openings. Add the washer to the back. Add a dab of glue to the screw holes and then insert the screws securely.

12 Fit the male part in the same way as for a regular magnetic snap. This is best done after constructing the bag if possible; this way you'll be able to mark where the female part sits when the bag is finished and place the male part accurately. Bend the prongs in on themselves.

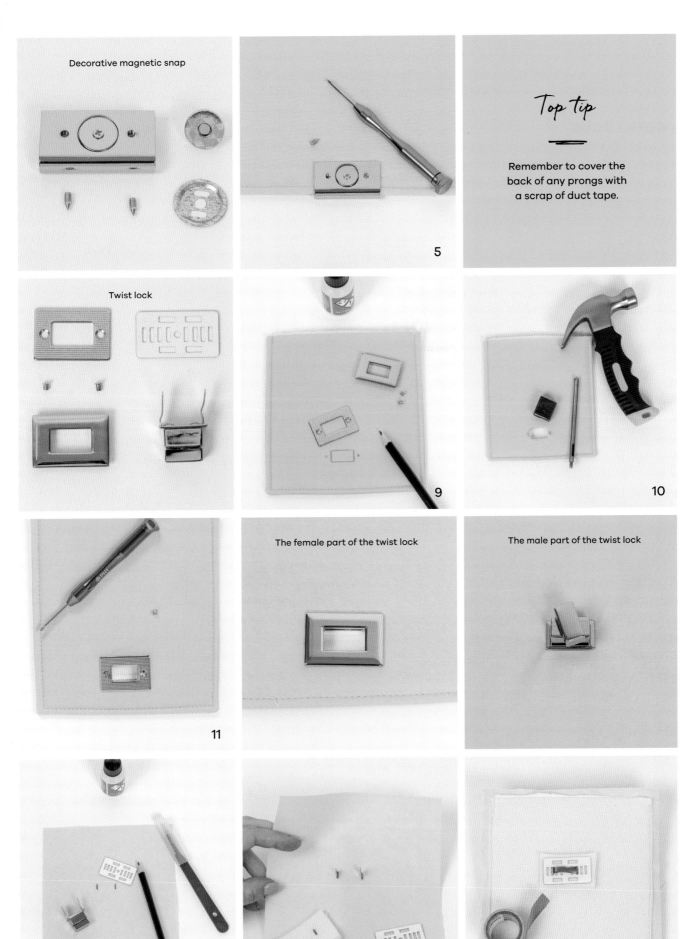

Decorative magnetic snap

Top tip

Remember to cover the
back of any prongs with
a scrap of duct tape.

5

Twist lock

9

10

11

The female part of the twist lock

The male part of the twist lock

12a

12b

12c

Press lock

PRESS LOCKS

Press locks are one of the most secure closures and are great for bags with a flap. They're easier to fit than twist locks, but do require a little clearance on the main bag for the female part to be fitted into place.

Usually the female part has prongs and the male part screws or prongs. Any prongs should come with a washer for fitting.

13 Finish the flap or pocket you'd like to add the male part to, then remove the screws and slot the male part onto the finished flap; mark the screw holes.

14 Using an awl, make two guide holes for the screws. Add a dab of glue and then insert the male part of the press lock. You may need to use the awl to encourage the fabric inside the channel of the press lock. Add the screws to the back and tighten.

13

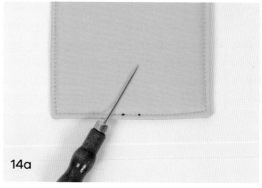

14a

14b

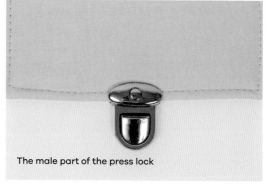

The male part of the press lock

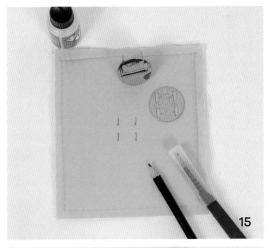

15

16a

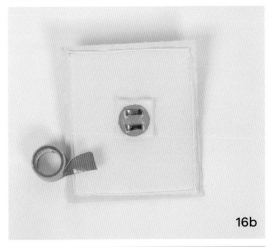

16b

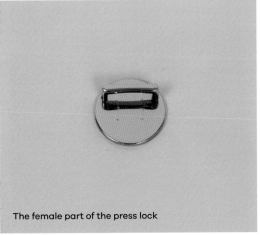

The female part of the press lock

15 Use the washer of the female part to mark where to create the slits for the prongs to slot through. This is best done after constructing the bag if possible; this way you'll be able to mark where the male part sits when the bag is finished and to place the female part accurately.

16 Fit the female part in the same way as for a regular magnetic snap. Remember to cover the back of any prongs with a scrap of duct tape.

RIVETS

Rivets can be used to secure pockets, add reinforcement to seams, secure layers that are too thick to sew and even close gaps where it's too tight to sew. One of our favourite retreat sayings is, 'stick a rivet in it', because it solves a multitude of bag making conundrums. Once you've mastered fitting rivets, you'll find that you incorporate them everywhere – even as decorative features on a flap.

Rivets are one of the hardware areas where you get what you pay for. It's a false economy to buy cheap rivets – you need to be able to rely on them to be able to carry the weight of the finished bag and your personal belongings, and to fit securely.

Double-cap rivets, which have a nicely finished cap on the underside of the post as well as on the top of the cap, are the most commonly used type of rivets. You can use them on finished panels, straps and flaps. Single-cap rivets have a hole under the post that will be mis-shapen after setting. They are only suitable for rivets in a panel where the underside will not be seen on the finished bag.

To determine what size of rivet to use, measure the thickness of the finished layers once compressed and choose the rivet post closest to that measurement.

Rivets are unlikely to set well on any surface with 'give', so a solid surface is a must. A thick kitchen chopping block on a work counter or a block of wood on a concrete floor are both great options. You are likely to punch holes into it, so ensure it's kept solely for fitting rivets.

To set rivets you will need a 2.5mm hole punch, a hammer, an anvil (the size should match the diameter of the rivet cap) and a setter (the size should match the diameter of the rivet cap).

17 Smooth the fabric over the solid surface, hold the hole punch upright in the desired position, and use short sharp taps with the hammer to punch the hole. Most rivets have a post diameter of 3mm (⅛in). It's best to punch a hole slightly smaller than this to ensure a tight fit.

18 Add a dab of Fray Check to the hole and push the rivet post through the hole.

19 Add the cap and listen for the 'click' that shows the cap is sitting tightly in the right place. This is not set but it is temporarily secure so if you have multiple rivets to set you can click them all into place before setting.

20 The anvil and setter each have a flat end and an end with a round dip. The round dip is for the rivet caps to sit inside, ensuring that the caps are not squashed in the setting process. To set the rivet, place the anvil with the inner dip facing up. Nestle the rivet cap into the anvil, then place the setter on top. Hold it at a set 90-degree angle, with the top rivet cap centred under the setter dip. Use short sharp taps with the hammer to set the rivet. Once you're happy that the rivet is set, check that there is no movement; you should not be able to feel any gap under the edge of the rivet.

Rivet setting tools

17

20

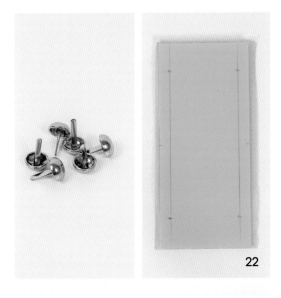

22

BAG FEET AND SOLID BASES

Bag feet are incredibly easy to install and add a professional finish to any bag. They are especially practical and help keep your beautiful handmade bag clean, even when it's placed on a restaurant floor or next to your desk at work. They can be installed without a solid base, but in a structured bag you may wish to add a solid base to ensure the bag maintains its shape even when loaded up.

21 Cut the bag base 1.2cm (½in) smaller than the finished base of the bag. Use the bag base to determine where and how many feet to add.

22 Punch a hole for each foot at least 1.2cm (½in) from each long edge of the solid bag base. Place the base on top of the exterior fabric, centre it and then mark through the holes to determine where to punch a hole for each foot. Add a dab of Fray Check to every hole.

23 For boxed-base bags, you may wish to determine the foot placement on the flat paper pattern, punch the holes, add Fray Check and then sew the bag. Remember to take the seam allowances into account when adding feet to a bag with a boxed base. Alternatively, sew the bag, box the corners and place the base on the outside to determine where to place the feet holes.

24 After the bag has been constructed, push the bag base through the turning gap in between the lining and exterior layers and add the feet by placing one hand inside the gap, one outside.

25 Push each foot through its hole, open the prongs out and add a scrap of duct tape to secure the prongs.

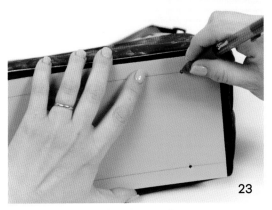

23

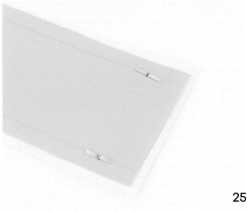

25

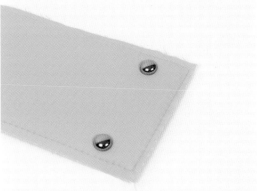

Bag base with feet in position

STRAP ANCHORS

For specific strap anchors, there are usually tutorials on the manufacturer's website with fitting instructions. I've detailed the most common below, because they add such a professional finish to a bag. They give a high-end designer look while being simple to fit.

It's worth checking the manufacturer's website for an installation template, although if a pattern calls for strap anchors you may find that the template is printed directly onto the pattern pieces.

You will be fitting strap anchors through exterior, interfacing and stabilizer layers to ensure that the bag can carry the weight of anything placed inside and that the fabric doesn't fail after installation.

STRAP ANCHORS WITH PRONGS

26 Using either an installation template or the washers, make four slits where the prongs should sit on the finished bag.

27 Snip through them, add a dab of Fray Check, and push the prongs through from the right side. Add a scrap of stabilizer followed by the washers. Bend the prongs in over themselves to secure and then add a scrap of duct tape to prevent them from rubbing through to any lining layers.

26

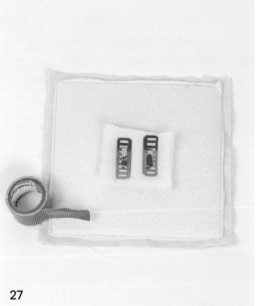

27

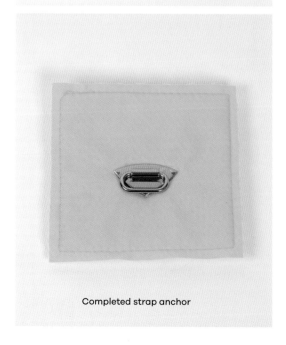

Completed strap anchor

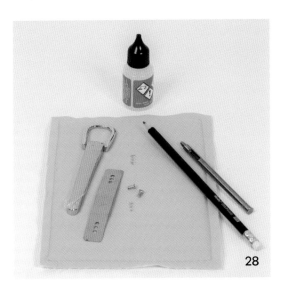

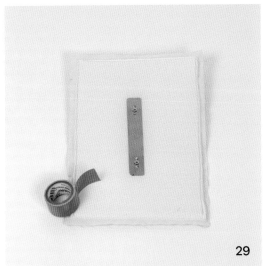

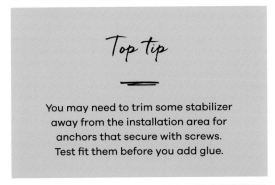

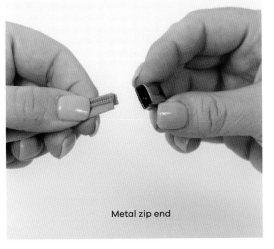

Metal zip end

STRAP ANCHORS WITH SCREWS

28 Using either an installation template or the washers, mark and make any holes indicated. Usually the washer will have extra holes punched with no screws. This is to help the anchor sit snugly into the fabric. Punch the holes through the fabric, using the washer holes for the placement.

29 Place the anchor right side up on top of the exterior fabric. Holding it in place, place it right side down on a soft surface to minimize scratches, then place the washer on the back over the pre-punched holes. Add a dab of glue to each screw hole and then tighten the screws into place.

BAG LABELS

It's so easy to add a bag label to your bag, and it really gives it a designer edge! Simply use the washer to mark where to cut the prong slits and then fit the label in the same way as a magnetic snap. Add a scrap of stabilizer to the back before you add the washer to ensure that it fits snugly to the exterior of the finished bag.

METAL ZIP END

A metal zip end is a great way to finish off the end of any kind of zip closure on the top of a bag. Trim the end of the zip tape to leave at least 2.5cm (1in), then fold the tape to the wrong side of the zip. Add a dab of glue into the zip end and push in the folded end of the zip before inserting the tiny fixing screw that comes with the zip end.

Top tip

You may need to trim some stabilizer away from the installation area for anchors that secure with screws. Test fit them before you add glue.

SCREW-TOGETHER ROUND GROMMETS

You can use regular grommets on your bags, but they are tricky to fit neatly. Screw-together grommets are simple to insert and look pretty.

30 The grommet is made of two parts – a grommet and a washer with screw holes. To fit screw-together grommets, first unscrew the two parts. Smooth all layers of the bag and insert a couple of pins outside the grommet placement area to keep all the layers together. To mark where to cut the hole, draw around the inside edge of the washer, as it's flat and won't move around. Mark and make the screw holes, too.

31 Add a thin line of Fray Check on the line on the right side of the bag, then carefully trim all layers to remove the fabric from within the hole placement area or use a shaped hole punch. Add Fray Check to all exposed edges of all layers of fabric, then slot the grommet in place from the right side.

32 Place some fabric on your work surface before leaning the grommet on it to prevent scratches, then add the back washer and screw it in place. It can be a good idea to add a thin line of glue to the hidden edge of the grommet before adding the back washer to ensure it doesn't work loose over time.

NOTE

For very large grommets such as those used as handles, it may be worth stitching around the outside of the hole placement line using a very scant 3mm (⅛in) seam allowance to ensure all of the layers are kept together and don't stretch over time.

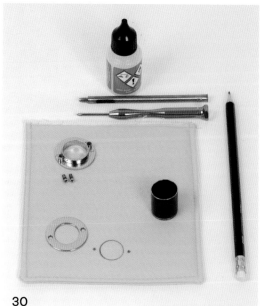

30

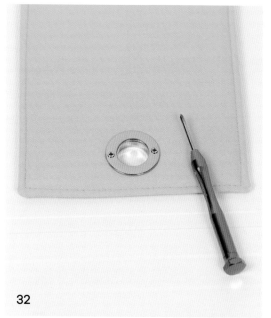

32

The completed grommet

Top tip

For a professional finish, choose strap hardware that perfectly matches the other hardware used on the bag.

STRAP HARDWARE

If you want to add an adjustable strap to your bag, you will need a strap slider and some means of attaching it. There is a wide range of rings and clips available for attaching straps to a bag. The ones listed here are the most common.

1 BRIDGE ANCHOR

A bridge anchor is a handy piece of hardware that allows you to add a D-ring where you may not wish to sew a tab – for example, in the centre of a panel or on the top of a flap. It comes with the bridge and a back washer. Some come with prongs that will need to be folded through the provided washer and some come with small screws that can be inserted into the washer. You will need to reinforce the area of insertion with some medium-weight interfacing and a heavy stabilizer such as foam or Decovil 1 to ensure that the weight of the hardware can be supported.

2 O-RING

An O-ring is a versatile connector that you can use on any straps or tabs where you may wish to add a swivel clip or just to split a strap into two sections for added interest. If you are not able to add it into a certain area, consider using a gate ring.

3 GATE RING

A gate ring is a regular O-shaped ring with a section that opens to allow it to be added to areas that may otherwise be inaccessible – for example, attaching a strap to a grommet or in the centre of a panel. They come both with hinged sections that may be fixed with a small screw and with sections that are completely removable and have two small screws.

4 SWIVEL CLIPS

These handy hooks have a bar at one end for a strap to fold through and a hook on the other to allow them to be connected to a ring of some kind. They're ideal for straps that may need to be removed, such as on clutches or convertible bags. Really small ones are also great for creating matching keyrings or tassels to accompany your finished bag!

5 RECTANGLE RING

A rectangle ring is a basic of strap making. You will need one to create a regular adjustable strap and you can use them to split straps for added interest. Check that the ring has the same finish as the strap slider so that your finished strap has a professional appearance. You can also use rectangle rings for strap tabs if no triangle rings are available, but be aware that they can twist and distort once a strap is added if you aren't able to sew extremely close to the ring.

6 STRAP SLIDER

A strap slider, sometimes called a triglide buckle or a strap buckle, is formed of a rectangular ring with a centre bar that can either be fixed in place or movable. Movable bars are better for thicker straps, but fixed bars may give a more high-end finish at times. It allows you to adjust the length of the strap. For details of how to attach a strap to a slider, *see Handles & Straps*.

7 TRIANGLE RING

You can use a triangle ring anywhere you need to connect a strip of fabric to a hook – for example, to attach a strap tab to a bag. Their unique shape prevents the bag from pulling on the strap tab and unsightly strap tab gathering as the contents of the bag move around.

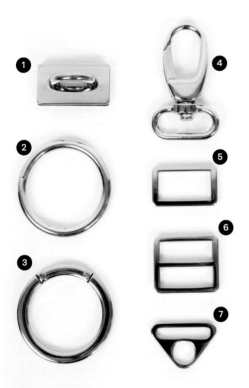

Handles & Straps

In this section, you'll find instructions for every strap and handle you can imagine. Customize any pattern by altering the straps and make the bag perfect for your needs.

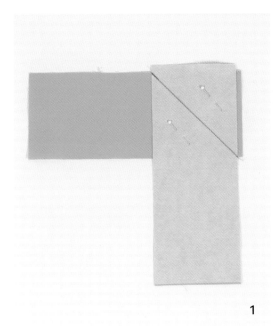

1

It's generally best to cut straps across the fabric to minimize stretch. However if you've chosen a non-woven interfacing (*see Tools & Materials: Interfacing and Stabilizers*) it will minimize stretch whichever way you cut the straps.

TO PIECE A STRAP

1 To piece a strap, place the ends of the two strap pieces right sides together at right angles, overlapping by 6mm (¼in), and stitch on a diagonal. Trim off the excess fabric, then press the seam open.

FOUR-FOLD STRAP

This is the most commonly used strap in bag making. To calculate the width of fabric, multiply the inside width of the strap hardware by four. A good elbow-length strap is usually 56cm (22in), shoulder-length 69cm (27in) and an adjustable crossbody strap 137–152cm (54–60in).

2 You'll need at least one finished end if you're going to be adding hardware. Fold the short end to the wrong side by 6mm (¼in) and press.

3 Fold the whole strap in half lengthwise and press. Open out, fold each long end in to the centre fold, and press.

4 Fold in half again along the original centre crease line, enclosing the long raw edges. Sew around all of the finished edges using a 3mm (⅛in) seam allowance.

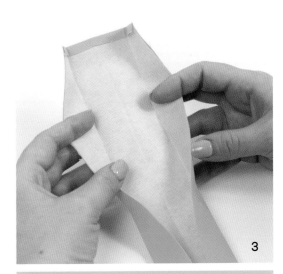

3

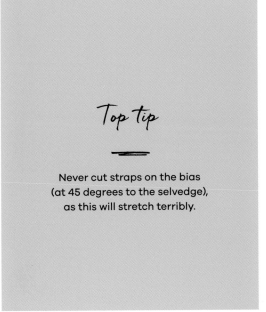

Top tip

——

Never cut straps on the bias (at 45 degrees to the selvedge), as this will stretch terribly.

TWO-TONE STRAP (FAUX PIPED STRAP)

A two-tone strap is an eye-catching way to upgrade your strap.

5 To sew a strap that appears as though it has been piped, cut two matching lengths of fabric – one twice the inside width of the strap hardware, the second 6mm (¼in) narrower than the first.

6 On the wrong side of the fabric, draw a line down the centre of both straps. Fold each long raw edge in to meet the centre line and press. For faux leather, glue and clip the folds rather than press them, as the fabric could melt from the heat of the iron.

7 Matching the short raw edges and centring the narrow strip on the wider one, place the straps right sides together and stitch along one end with a scant 6mm (¼in) seam allowance.

8 Turn the strap right side out and press well using a pressing cloth. Clip the edges together.

9 Topstitch along both long edges and the finished short edge 3mm (⅛in) from the edge.

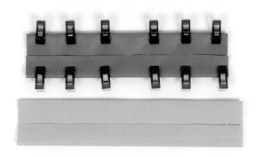

6

7

9

11

FULLY ENCLOSED STRAP

A fully enclosed strap is perfect for a handle or strap that won't be sewn into the side seams of a bag. All raw edges will be hidden in the strap, resulting in a professional finish. This is great for a removable adjustable strap with a swivel clip on either end.

10 Cut the strap four times the inside width of the strap hardware.

11 Fold the strap in half lengthwise, wrong sides together, and press. Unfold. Fold each long raw edge in to meet the centre crease line and press.

12 Fold the strap in half, back on itself along the centre crease (so the raw edges are out). Stitch along both short edges with a 6mm (¼in) seam allowance.

13 Trim the corners of the short edges, turn right side out, and tuck the raw edges inside. Push the corners out and then press well.

14 Topstitch all around 3mm (⅛in) from the edge, starting with the open edge.

12

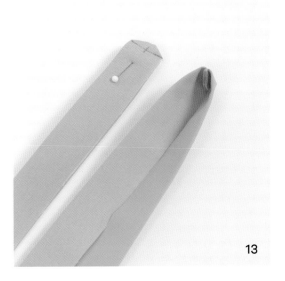

13

FIXED ADJUSTABLE STRAP

This is the most common type of adjustable strap and works well on most shoulder and crossbody bags. You will need a strap slider and rectangle ring with the same internal width.

15 To make a strap that will be sandwiched between the exterior and the lining, you will need to cut one strap and one strap tab. Cut the strap four times the internal width of the strap slider and cut the strap tab twice the internal width of the matching rectangle ring. Generally I like to cut my straps 152cm (60in) long and my strap tabs 15.5cm (6in) long; this makes a comfortable length for most wearers.

16 Fold each long raw edge of the strap tab in to the centre and press. Topstitch along the two long edges, stitching 3mm (⅛in) from the edge, then fold the strap tab in half over the bar of the rectangle ring and stitch or rivet to secure.

17 The strap will need one finished end; you may wish to use the Fully Enclosed Strap method on just one end of the strap. Fold 2.5cm (1in) of the enclosed end of the strap over the centre bar of the strap slider and stitch it in place. You may want to add a rivet to secure. If the strap slider has a right side, it should be facing up.

18 Thread the loose end of the strap over the bar of the rectangle ring on the short strap tab. If the rectangle ring has a right side, it should be facing up.

19 Thread the end of the strap through the strap slider buckle over the previously stitched end and out the other side.

20 Stitch the ends of the adjustable strap to the centre sides of the bag exterior within the seam allowance, with the 'wrong' side of the strap facing up. Take care not to twist the strap.

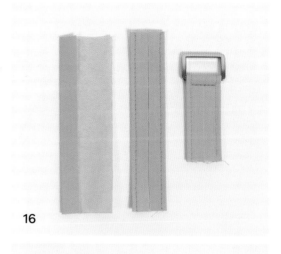

16

17

18

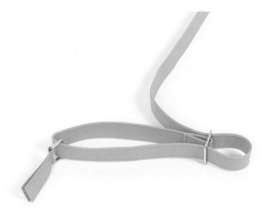

19

23

24

Top tip

To make an adjustable strap with a ring on each end, follow the above method and substitute rings for the swivel clips.

27

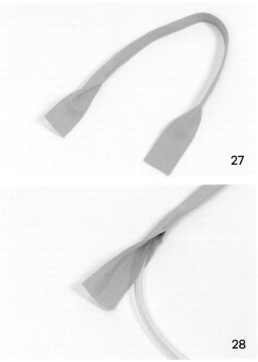

28

REMOVABLE ADJUSTABLE STRAP

A removable adjustable strap is a great option for clutch bags or bags with short handles that benefit from a second strap. You will need a strap slider and two swivel clips with the same internal widths.

21 To make a strap that will have two swivel clips and can be completely removable, you will only need to cut and sew one strap; make it fully enclosed.

22 Thread one end of the finished strap through the strap slider, fold over 2.5cm (1in) and stitch to secure, as for the fixed adjustable strap. Add a rivet if you wish. If the strap slider has a right side, it should be facing up.

23 Thread the other end of the strap through one swivel clip, and then back through the strap slider over the end you secured in the previous step.

24 Thread the strap end through the second swivel clip, fold over 2cm (¾in), then stitch to secure. Add a rivet if you wish.

ROLLED HANDLES

Rolled handles are great for bags designed to carry heavier items, as they fit comfortably in your hand, making them a pleasure to hold. To make rolled handles you will need plastic tubing 8mm (⅜in) in diameter, although this can sometimes be omitted on narrower handles as the bulk of the fabric will create the 'roll' on the handle.

25 To use plastic tubing, cut two pieces of fabric and two of medium-weight interfacing (*see Tools & Materials: Interfacing and Stabilizers*) 7cm (2¾in) wide x your chosen length, then fuse the interfacing to each fabric piece.

26 Draw a line lengthwise down the centre of the handles, fold each long edge to the centre line and press. Topstitch along both long edges 2mm (a scant ⅛in) from the edge. Fold the handles in half again, matching the folded edges, and clip to secure in place.

27 Make a mark where you would like the tubing to start and end, then sew between the two marks using a 2mm (a scant ⅛in) seam allowance. Cut the tubing 2.5cm (1in) shorter than this section.

28 Push the tubing into the channel you've just sewn until it's centred in the handle.

29 Attach the handles to the bag panels using a 3mm (⅛in) seam allowance, stitching along each edge and as close to the tubing as possible.

NOTE

You may wish to turn under a 6mm (¼in) hem on each short end of rolled handles if the handle ends will not be sewn directly into a seam.

Piping

Piping is a great way to lift a handmade bag and add extra interest. It gives a professional finish without adding weight or bulk. This section will show you how to make your own piping and apply it to your bag, whether it's along a pocket top or a flap or around a curved gusset. You'll need an adjustable piping/zipper foot (*see Tools & Materials: Machine Feet*), some double-sided basting tape, a small ruler and an erasable fabric marker.

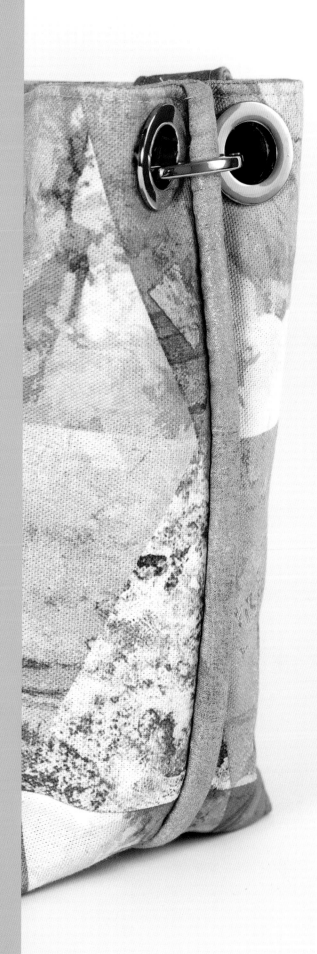

2

4

MAKING PIPING

Choose the size of piping cord to suit the project: on smaller bags, a more delicate piping is usually chosen, but chunky piping can have great impact!

1 Steam press the piping cord and piping fabric before starting. Cord is usually 100% cotton and can shrink later, creating unsightly wrinkles.

2 To determine the width of the piping fabric, measure the circumference of the cord by wrapping a soft tape measure around it, then add twice the seam allowance of the bag you'll be sewing it to; 1cm (⅜in) is a common seam allowance for bags. Cut the piping fabric on the bias (at a 45-degree angle) as long as you can, and to the width required.

3 If you need to join pieces of piping fabric together to get the required length, *see Handles & Straps: To Piece a Strap*.

4 Wrap the piping fabric around the piping cord, matching the long raw edges, and pin or clip to hold the edges together. Sew reasonably close to the piping cord, using a long machine tacking (basting) stitch; you may want to use a matching thread colour to ensure these stitches are not visible.

Top tip

Before using pre-made piping, cut a length longer than you think you will need and steam press it. This will help it to shrink, if it's going to, before you apply it to your panel.

PIPING A STRAIGHT SECTION

5 Measure the seam allowance of the piping, then compare that to the seam allowance of the pattern you're following. The difference between them is how far from the edge of the panel you'll need to place the raw edge of the piping. If the piping seam allowance is smaller than the panel seam allowance, you'll need to draw a line at the distance between the two. For example, if the bag seam allowance is 1cm (⅜in) and the piping only has a 6mm (¼in) seam allowance, draw a line 3mm (⅛in) from the edge of the panel. If the piping seam allowance is larger, trim it down to match the seam allowance of the pattern.

6 Apply a line of double-sided basting tape along the edge of the line you've just drawn, on the side nearest the bulk of the fabric.

7 Align the raw edge of the piping with the line you've drawn on the fabric, place the piping on the basting tape and press down to secure. If the seam allowance of the piping matches the pattern, then match the raw edge of the piping to the raw edge of the panel.

8 Using a long stitch length, machine tack (baste) along the piping, stitching as close to the cord as possible without stitching over the cord.

9 Place the second piece of fabric on top, right sides together, sandwiching the piping in between, and pin or clip to hold the layers in place.

10 Turn the panel over so that the machine tacking stitches are on top, and change the stitch length back to your usual length. Sew exactly on top of the tacking stitches.

11 If the piping is at the edge of a flap or pocket, turn the fabric wrong sides together, with the piping protruding, and press well. If the piping seems to want to 'roll', use pins to keep the fabric edges together. Topstitch 3mm (⅛in) from the fabric edge.

5–7

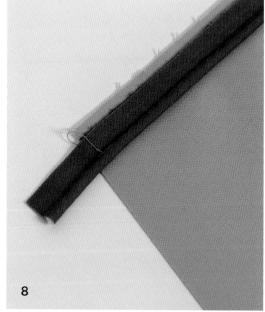

8

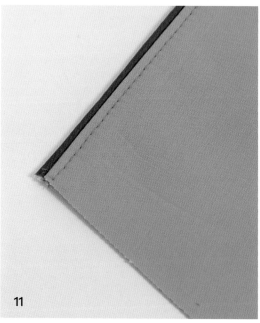

11

PIPING A CURVED SECTION

12 Follow steps 5-7 of Piping a Straight Section to determine where to place the piping.

13 Choose where you want the piping to start and angle the end to run off into the seam allowance. Where the piping goes into the seam allowance, you can cut off the cord from inside if you wish.

14 Start to apply the piping to the basting tape and continue along the panel until you reach a curve. Snip into the seam allowance of the piping, ensuring that you don't snip too close to the cord.

15 Manipulate the piping around the curve, pulling it to sit neatly on the line you've drawn. You may need to stretch it slightly to sit neatly around the curves.

16 When you reach the starting point, again angle the end to run off into the seam allowance, creating a small X of piping crossing the line you've drawn. Where the piping goes into the seam allowance, you can cut off the cord from inside if you wish.

17 Using a long stitch length, machine tack (baste) along the piping, stitching as close to the cord as possible without stitching over the cord.

18 When you need to sew another panel to this one, turn the panels over so that the tacking stitches are on top and change the stitch length back to your usual length. Sew exactly on top of the tacking stitches.

ADDING PIPING TO A BAG WITH A GUSSET

When sewing a bag with a gusset, I find that it's always best to sew with the gusset on top, rather than the main panel. It results in a neater finish, with fewer gusset puckers. It's best to apply the piping to the long raw edges of the gusset, so that the tacking (basting) stitches are visible.

USING A ZIP AS PIPING

For a fun alternative, why not try using zip teeth as piping? Simply cut a length of zip, separate the teeth and then use in the same way as piping, making sure that the zip teeth and exterior fabric are right sides together.

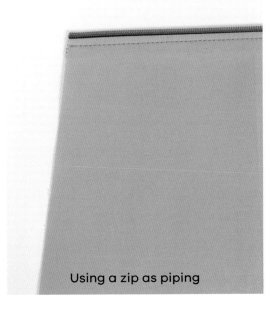

Using a zip as piping

Shaping

Adding shape and depth to a bag is easy and it adds so much to the finish of the design. This section will talk you through the most common methods.

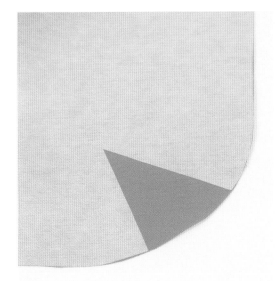

1

DARTS

Darts give a bag a softer, more rounded feel at the base while still adding practical depth.

1 It's a good idea to cut the interfacing away from the dart lines when cutting out, as this makes it easier to line them up during construction. Alternatively, trace the dart lines from the pattern piece onto the wrong side of the main panels. Stitch along both dart lines to the point; this will compress any stabilizer or interfacing and allow the fabric to fold naturally along the dart lines.

2 Fold the fabric right sides together, matching the dart lines, and run a small blunt tool along the inside of the dart to ensure that the fabric hasn't puckered or creased when it was folded.

3 Pin the dart. Starting at the edge of the fabric, sew along the dart lines to the dart point, without backstitching. Instead, leave the thread tails long and tie them off.

3

GUSSETS

To double check the length of the gusset, use a length of bias binding (*see Resizing: Bags with a Gusset*); this will help ensure a great finish.

4 To apply a gusset to a bag, pin or clip the centre of the gusset to the centre of the main panel, right sides together.

5 Pin or clip each end of the gusset to the top edge of the main panel.

6 Next, work your way along the straight edges of the main panel, pinning or clipping the gusset in place.

7 Once you've pinned all the straight edges in place, ease the gusset around any curves. You may need to make small snips into the seam allowance of the gusset to allow it to stretch around any curves, or to sit neatly.

8 Sew with the gusset on top, then trim the seam allowances of the curves with pinking shears, or clip into the seam allowances of all layers, to remove bulk and allow the fabric inside the curve to sit neatly once turned through.

7

BOXED CORNERS

Boxed corners are one of the most popular methods of adding depth to a bag. They create a neat finish and a squared base shape, enabling the bag to stand up on its own.

REGULAR BOXED CORNERS

9 Sew the main panels of the bag right sides together along the side and bottom edges. If possible, press the seams open. The easiest way to do this is to fold back one side of the seam and press it, then turn the piece over and press the second side.

10 Pull the main panels out at an angle to bring the side seam to meet the bottom seam. This will mean that the previously straight corners are now pointed out at an angle.

11 Pop a pin through the side seam. Looking inside the bag and using the pin as a guide, match the side and bottom seams.

12 Pin or clip the seams in place, then measure across the point, at 90 degrees to the seam, to determine where to sew. For a 10cm (4in) depth, the line intersecting the point should measure 10cm (4in). You can easily alter the depth of a bag by altering this line (*see Resizing: Bags with Boxed Corners*). Sew directly on the marked line, backstitching at each end.

9

12

Top tip

When sewing, you may wish to sew a second line of stitching across the corner to reduce strain on the boxed corner; this will prevent unsightly stitches from showing from the wrong side on bulky fabrics.

13

14

16

17

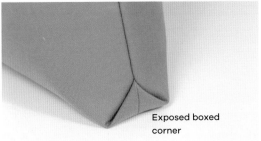

Exposed boxed corner

CUT-OUT BOXED CORNERS

You can make any boxed corner a cut-out boxed corner by trimming away the fabric from the bottom corners of a bag. Many people find cut-out boxed corners easier to sew, as you can keep an eye on the layers inside the boxing and align the seams more easily.

13 Usually the pattern will have the corners cut out already or direct you to cut out the corners. If it doesn't, you will need to cut away half the finished depth. For example, for a 10cm (4in) deep bag, cut 5cm (2in) away from each bottom corner. Ignore any seam allowances; as long as you sew the side/bottom seams with the same seam allowance as you use to sew the boxed corner, they will cancel each other out and you will end up with a perfectly sized boxed corner.

14 Sew as for a regular boxed corner, but when matching the side and bottom seams, also match the raw edges of the corner cut-outs. Remember to backstitch at the start of the stitching on each cut-out boxed corner. Sew along the corners using the seam allowance specified in the pattern. You may wish to sew over the ends of the previous seams a couple of times to ensure they're secure.

EXPOSED BOXED CORNERS

These are a fun alteration to regular boxed corners, but can only be added to bags that have a 90-degree corner. The exposed corner will be sewn into the side seam and may not catch on an angled bag. It's best to remove the stabilizer from the corners on the exterior panels by cutting it away; for 5cm (2in) corners, cut away 6.5cm (2½in) of stabilizer to allow the fabric to fold easily.

15 The bottom seam will need to be folded up into a 'W' shape and sandwiched between the side seams. To determine how far to fold, decide on the finished depth of the bag and then divide by two. Don't worry about any creasing of the fabric against the stabilizer while folding – as long as the fabric is smooth at the seam line, you will end up with a great boxed corner.

16 Sew the bottom seam only of the bag, then fold one panel so that the top raw edge is half the finished depth of the boxed corner from the second top raw edge.

17 Turn the panel over, then repeat the fold so that both top raw edges are now at the same level.

18 Sew along both long side edges, sandwiching the bottom seam between them. When the bag is turned right side out, these triangles of fabric will settle into corners, giving you exposed boxed corners.

Resizing

Make your handmade bag the perfect size for your needs! This section contains all the techniques you will need to resize patterns of all shapes and sizes. You will need spare paper, pattern to alter, calculator, paper scissors, adhesive tape, a pen or pencil, a ruler and bias binding.

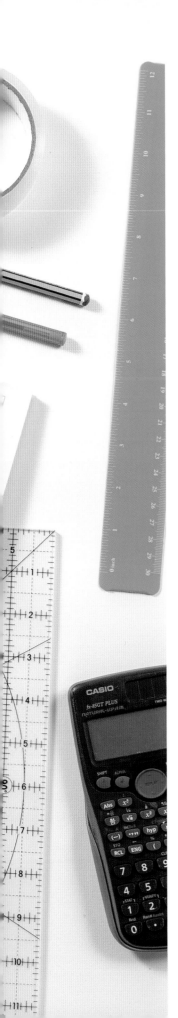

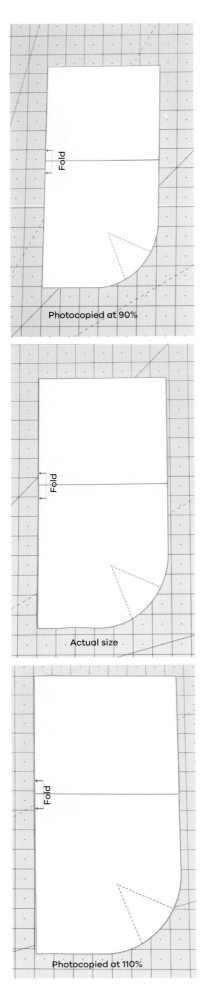

Fold

Photocopied at 90%

Fold

Actual size

Fold

Photocopied at 110%

SIMPLE SHAPES AND BAGS WITH DARTED BASES

To alter the size of a simple bag or a bag with a darted base, simply print or photocopy the pattern at a different percentage, remembering to resize all of the pieces at that different size. To calculate the percentage you need, use the following formula:

Desired Dimension (DD) divided by Original Dimension (OD) multiplied by 100

DD / OD x 100

For example, if the original pattern is 25.5cm (10in) wide, and you want to end up with a width of 23cm (9in), photocopy or print the pattern at 90%. If you want the finished width to be 28cm (11in), photocopy or print the pattern at 110%.

BAGS WITH BOXED CORNERS

To alter the size of a bag's boxed corners when no other changes are required, then it's advisable to alter the dimensions manually. To change a boxed base from a finished depth of 12.5cm (5in) to 15cm (6in), just add 1.2cm (½in) to each side of the corner cut-outs within the pattern.

1 First, identify if there is a point at which the pattern piece needs to remain unchanged. The bag pictured here uses a frame, so the dimensions above this point need to remain the same.

2 Attach the pattern piece to some spare paper, allowing extra on each side that will need to be altered – usually the base and side.

3 Next, draw a line extending from the corner cut-outs to the desired depth. I've added 1.2cm (½in) on both sides. The bottom of my spare paper will be 1.2cm (½in) from the bottom of the pattern piece.

4 Draw a new line from the side extension to a natural point near the top, as pictured. This will give you a bag that has the same width and height as one made from the original pattern, but with the new depth.

5 If you want to alter the width, then add extra width from the fold line or from the centre, as detailed below.

BAGS WITH A GUSSET

To alter a bag with a gusset, it's advisable to alter the pattern pieces. Not every dimension will be suitable for increasing or decreasing, but using this method you can alter only those dimensions that you want to change.

6 First, find the centre of the main panel, then increase or decrease from there. To increase the width, add spare paper to the centre line. If this is a fold line, simply tape the extra width to the fold line. I like to cut a spare piece of paper to the desired width plus 1.2cm (½in) and then draw a line at 1.2cm (½in) that I can use as a guideline for positioning the extra paper.

7 Tape the paper behind the existing pattern piece, with the original edge along the 1.2cm (½in) drawn line.

8 If you also want to alter the height, fold the pattern piece in half to find the centre line and mark with a pencil.

NOTE

Remember that adding width at a fold line will double the added amount.

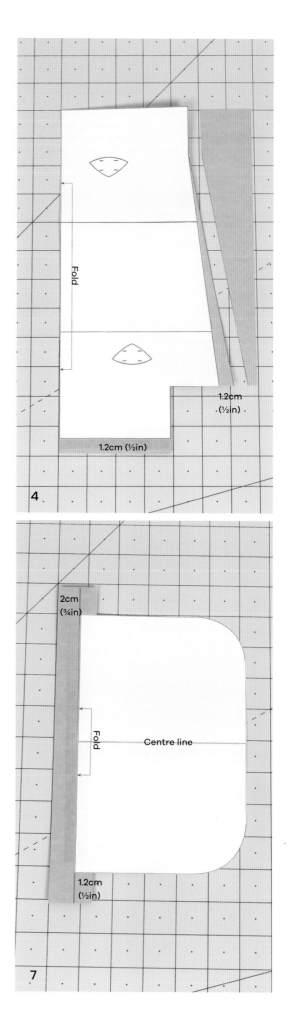

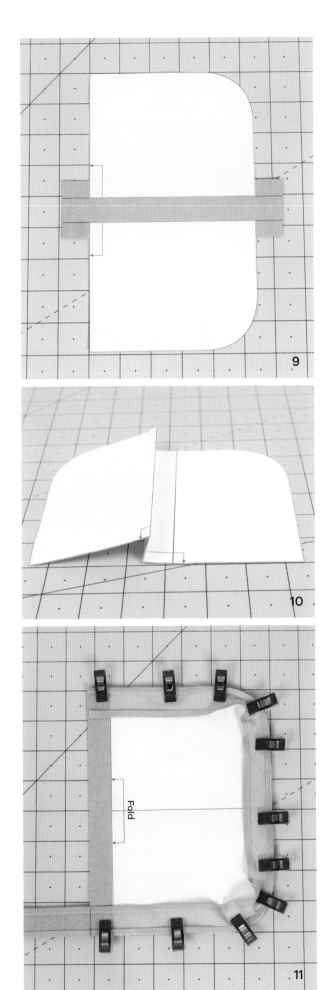

9 To increase the height, cut along the centre line and add spare paper behind to add the extra height desired.

10 To decrease the height, calculate half the desired height change and draw a line this distance from the centre line, both above and below. So for a 5cm (2in) decrease in height, draw a line 2.5cm (1in) above and 2.5cm (1in) below the centre line. Fold the pattern piece so that the bottom line meets the top line and tape in place.

11 In theory, you will simply need to add or subtract the same amount to each gusset piece. In practice, you need to double check! Cut a long piece of bias tape. Starting at the centre bottom, clip or pin the tape around the perimeter of the bag, easing it as you go. This will move around corner curves in the same way as a clipped gusset, so it's great for measuring. Finish at the centre top point and mark the tape. Unclip the bias tape, lay it out flat and measure the length. This will give you the length of your finished gusset.

12 Double check that adding or subtracting to the gusset pieces will result in this length of gusset; if it does not, then alter the pattern as necessary. Don't forget to take seam allowances into account!

Professional touches

This section will show you some tips that you can use to make your bag look more professional. The end result starts at the very beginning.

1

PREPARING THE FABRIC

Unless you're going to wash your bag or you have a sensitivity to the chemicals used in the fabric manufacturing process, there's absolutely no need to wash fabric before you use it for bag making. If you do wash it, you can use a spray starch or similar to get a super-smooth finish to the fabric before you start cutting.

A fabric washed on a vigorous spin cycle can result in stubborn creases that remain no matter what you do, ending with a creased bag.

If you don't pre-wash the fabric, steam press it before you work with it to ensure that any shrinkage is dealt with before you apply any fusible interfacings.

PATTERN MATCHING

If the fabric you're using has a pattern or stripe, then try to match these when cutting. I find the easiest way to do this is to cut the pattern pieces out from interfacing first and mark on the interfacing where certain designs/stripes are before fusing.

1 When trying to pattern match a pocket, cut the main panel piece first, then lay the pocket interfacing glue side up on top and draw over a few prominent features of the pattern using a removable marker.

2 Turn the interfacing over, so that it's glue side down. Place it on the wrong side of the patterned fabric, carefully matching up the marks you made with the pattern on the fabric. Fuse in place, then cut out the pocket piece.

2

Top tip

If you have fabric with a particular design feature or motif that you would like to highlight, why not cut the interfacing first? Then you can choose where to position it, fuse it in place and cut around the outside of the interfacing.

TURNING GAPS

3 To get a really neat turning gap, whether it's on a pocket or the main bag, sew across the gap with a long stitch length (such as 5.0). Then steam press and remove the stitches. You'll be left with a neat line of stitch holes.

4 Finger press or steam press along these holes to help the seam allowances turn under neatly.

For a really great hidden turning gap, leave a turning gap in both the bottom of a zip pocket and the bottom of a bag lining. Turn the bag through the larger bag lining hole to reduce creases in the main bag. Reach through the zipped pocket turning gap to gain access to the wrong sides of the main bag lining. Stitch the turning gap closed and then push back through the zipped pocket.

Now you can close the zipped pocket turning gap before tucking it back inside the zipped pocket. This will not only reduce creases from the final turn but also make it far easier to turn the bag through.

NEAT CORNERS

For really neat corners, sew the seams and then cut across the corner at a 45-degree angle. Cut into the seam allowance again, above and below the corner at an angle, to ensure that as little fabric as possible is in each finished corner (*see photo*).

WELL-FITTING LININGS

For a really well-fitting lining, stitch the first and last 2.5cm (1in) using the seam allowance specified in the pattern (which is normally 1cm/⅜in), but increase to 1.2cm (½in) in between (*see photo*). Make sure that the first and last 2.5cm (1in) match the exterior seam allowances, so that they fit when the lining and exterior are joined together.

You can also add a few hand stitches 'in the ditch' through the exterior seam to the lining to hold each area in place.

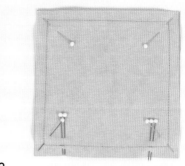

3

4

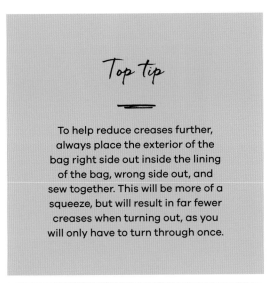

Top tip

To help reduce creases further, always place the exterior of the bag right side out inside the lining of the bag, wrong side out, and sew together. This will be more of a squeeze, but will result in far fewer creases when turning out, as you will only have to turn through once.

DEALING WITH BULK

Don't be afraid to show your bag who's boss! To begin with, trim any heavy stabilizer from areas that will be bulky at the end. Trim 1.2cm (½in) squares from each boxed corner seam and any top side seams. As long as the stabilizer is still caught in two seams, there should be no issues with it shifting.

Press open any seams that are bulky and thick and consider giving them either a good whack with a non-marking white mallet, or use a piece of calico and a hammer. If you don't want the neighbours to think there's something wrong, then a tailor's clapper with steam will help flatten bulk pretty well.

To start stitching onto very thick layers, you might find that a hump jumper or a wedge of folded paper placed at the back of the walking foot can help maintain a level foot and a great start to the topstitching. As you sew it'll fall away, so you don't need to worry about stopping to remove it.

And finally, if the seam you wish to topstitch is just far too thick, consider topstitching between seams only and using a rivet where necessary.

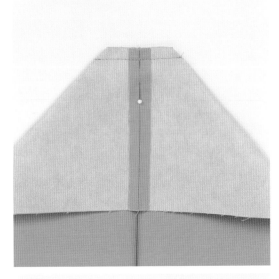

THE IMPORTANCE OF STEAM

Throughout the entire bag making process you will find that if you stop at each step and press if necessary you will have a great finish at the end – whether that's pressing pockets, pressing seam allowances open or pressing tabs and handles.

For super-neat boxed corners, press open the side and bottom seam allowances before boxing. If that's not possible, then press open at least the end 5cm (2in), using the narrow end of an ironing board or a sleeve board (*see photo*).

Make sure you're using a hard surface to press on. If you find you're not getting a great finish, then consider using a tailor's clapper – a wooden tool that you can use to 'beat' steam through a seam and encourage it to sit flat (*see Tools & Materials: Tools*).

TOPSTITCHING

Use at least a 3.0 stitch length for topstitching, if not 3.5. This slightly longer stitch length looks neater and, if you can maintain the same stitch length for all of the topstitching throughout the bag, then it'll look pulled together and cohesive.

Don't fall into the trap of sewing too slowly to get a good straight stitch line: sometimes sewing too slowly can make you wobble a bit more than usual! Choose a good, even pace that you're able to maintain. If you need to adjust your hands on the fabric, then slow to a stop, reposition and then begin again. Adjusting whilst sewing can result in a wobble!

And finally, resist backstitching when topstitching. Instead, leave the thread tails long and use a pin to tease the front thread through to the bobbin side, where you can double knot and then trim (*see photo*).

Projects

The Piped Hobo

This beginner-friendly hobo bag is a great way to show off a signature print. With chunky side piping and some really special bling, it is perfect for everyday wear or a stylish work situation.

FABRICS USED

Thomas Home Décor Triangles, Blue Grey and Grunge Metallic Grey Couture

SKILL LEVEL

Beginner

YOU WILL NEED

Fabrics

0.75m (⅞yd) exterior fabric

1m (1⅛yd) lining fabric

2m (2¼yd) medium-weight interfacing, 90cm (1yd) wide; narrower interfacing will need more

1m (1⅛yd) fusible fleece, 72cm (28in) wide; narrower fleece will need more

NOTE

These amounts are for non-directional fabrics; directional fabrics may need more.

Notions

1 x 20cm (8in) #3 zip to match lining fabric

1 x 14mm (⁹⁄₁₆in) slim magnetic snap

53cm (21in) piping cord/rope, 1cm (⅜in) diameter

4 x 20mm (¾in) screw-together round grommets

2 x 38mm (1½in) gate rings

1 x 30mm (1¼in) strap slider

FINISHED SIZE (W x H x D)

32 x 25 x 18cm (12½ x 10 x 7in)

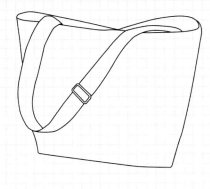

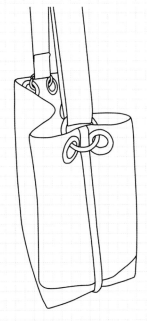

CUTTING INSTRUCTIONS

All measurements are given as width x height. A seam allowance of 1cm (⅜in) is included.

FROM EXTERIOR FABRIC

- For A (Adjustable Strap), cut one piece 12.5 x 112cm (5 x 44in)

- For B (Main Panels), cut two pieces 45 x 38cm (18 x 15in)

FROM LINING FABRIC

- For B (Main Panels), cut two pieces 45 x 38cm (18 x 15in)

- For C (Slip Pockets and Zip Pocket), cut three pieces 25.5 x 30.5cm (10 x 12in)

- For D (Chunky Piping), cut two pieces 30.5cm (12in) high x the diameter of the cord + 2cm (¾in); there's no need to cut this on the bias (*see Piping: Making Piping*)

FROM MEDIUM-WEIGHT INTERFACING

- For A (Adjustable Strap), cut one piece 12.5 x 112cm (5 x 44in)

- For B (Main Panels), cut two pieces 45 x 38cm (18 x 15in)

- For C (Slip Pockets and Zip Pocket), cut three pieces 25.5 x 30.5cm (10 x 12in)

FROM FUSIBLE FLEECE

- For B (Main Panels), cut two pieces 45 x 38cm (18 x 15in)

STABILIZERS

1 Fuse medium-weight interfacing to all pieces. Fuse fusible fleece to the exterior main panels (B) – *see Tools & Materials: Interfacing and Stabilizers*.

2 Cut a 7.5cm (3in) square from each bottom corner of the exterior and lining main panels (B).

Top tip

You will find it helpful to mark the centres of all pieces on the top and bottom edges within the seam allowance.

LINING CONSTRUCTION

3 Using the 20cm (8in) #3 zip and one (C) panel, make a zip pocket and insert it into one lining main panel (B), making the box 20cm (8in) long and positioning it 12.5cm (5in) from the bottom edge of the zip pocket (see *Pockets: Simple Zip Pocket*). Place the bottom edge of the zip pocket 16.5cm (6½in) from the bottom edge of the panel. Once you've sewn the zip pocket in place, pin it up and out of the way. Don't forget to leave a turning gap in the bottom of the pocket for turning the bag through.

4 Using the remaining (C) pieces, make two simple slip pockets (see *Pockets: Simple Slip Pocket*). Attach the slip pockets to the lining main panels (B), placing them 10cm (4in) from the bottom of the lining panels and centred on the width, dividing them if you wish (see *Pockets: Divided Slip Pocket*). Unpin the zip pocket after attaching the slip pocket.

5 Attach a magnetic snap to each lining main panel (B), positioning the top edge of the washer 2.5cm (1in) from the top edge of the lining main panel and centred on the width (see *Hardware & Bling: Regular Magnetic Snaps*).

6 Place the two lining main panels (B) right sides together and sew along the sides and bottom edges, leaving the corner cut-outs open (see *Professional Touches: Well-fitting Linings*).

7 Press open the side and bottom seams, then box the corners (see *Shaping: Cut-out Boxed Corners*).

The lining construction is finished for now and can be placed to one side.

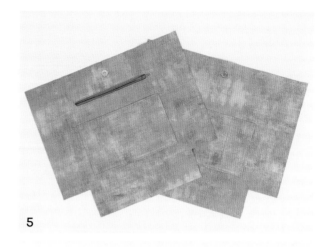

5

7

9

EXTERIOR CONSTRUCTION

8 Using the chunky piping pieces (D), create two lengths of piping (*see Piping: Making Piping*). Cut the piping cord into two 26.5cm (10½in) lengths and centre each one in a length of piping. The seam allowance on the flange should be 1cm (⅜in).

9 Place a line of double-sided basting tape along the left-hand edge of one exterior main panel (B), on the right side of the fabric. Place the piping on top, matching the raw edges. Tack (baste) the piping in place, then repeat for the second exterior main panel.

10 Place the exterior main panels (B) right sides together and sew along the side and bottom edges, leaving the corner cut-outs open. Sew the sides with the piping tacking stitches facing up, using a 1cm (⅜in) seam allowance.

11 Press open the side and bottom seams, then box the corners (*see Shaping: Cut-out Boxed Corners*).

12 Place the exterior inside the lining, right sides together and matching the side seams, and sew around the top edge. Turn through the gap in the bottom of the zip pocket and then stitch the gap closed.

13 Press the top of the bag well and topstitch around the top of the bag 3mm (⅛in) from the edge, without stitching over the piping.

FINISH THE BAG

14 Smooth the top of the bag. On both sides of the bag, insert a screw-together grommet through all layers (*see Hardware & Bling: Screw-together Round Grommets*).

15 Thread the gate rings through the grommets.

16 Using piece A, make a fully enclosed strap (*see Handles & Straps: Fully Enclosed Strap*). Attach the strap to the bag using the strap slider and gate rings (*see Handles & Straps: Removable Adjustable Strap*).

12

14

15

The Celebration
CLUTCH

With this simple and classy clutch, you're ready
to attend any social occasion. Whether it's
a garden party, afternoon tea or a night out
painting the town red with the girls, it's the
perfect accessory – the cleverly planned interior
ensures that you won't have to rummage around
to find your favourite things.

FABRICS USED

Meraki Nefertari Marzipan and From Old Harry Rocks Gentle Waves on Light Aqua

SKILL LEVEL

Advanced beginner

YOU WILL NEED

Fabrics

60 x 60cm (24 x 24in) exterior fabric

60 x 60cm (24 x 24in) lining fabric

60 x 25cm (24 x 10in) single-sided fusible Decovil 1 or Peltex

75cm (30in) medium-weight interfacing, 90cm (1yd) wide

NOTE

You may wish to turn under a 6mm (¼in) hem on each short end of rolled handles if the handle ends will not be sewn directly into a seam.

Notions

1 x 15cm (6in) #3 zip to match lining fabric

2 x 14mm (⁹⁄₁₆in) slim magnetic snaps

Double-sided basting tape

FINISHED SIZE (W x H x D)

23 x 24 x 4cm (9 x 9½ x 1½in)

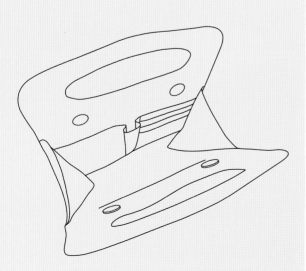

CUTTING INSTRUCTIONS

All measurements are given as width x height. A seam allowance of 1cm (⅜in) is included.

FROM EXTERIOR FABRIC:

- For A (Main Body), cut one using pattern piece A
- For B (Gussets), cut two using pattern piece B
- For C (Handle Facings), cut two pieces 20 x 9cm (8 x 3½in)

FROM LINING FABRIC:

- For A (Main Body), cut one using pattern piece A
- For B (Gussets), cut two using pattern piece B
- For C (Handle Facings), cut two pieces 20 x 9cm (8 x 3½in)
- For D (Card Holder), cut one piece 11.5 x 37cm (4½ x 14¾in)
- For E (Slip and Lipbalm Pockets), cut one piece 18 x 10.5cm (7 x 4¼in)
- For F (Pocket Backing), cut one piece 28 x 10.5cm (11 x 4¼in)
- For G (Zip Pocket) – this comprises pieces G1, G2 and G3
    - For G1 (Zip Pocket Facing), cut one piece 20 x 3.5cm (8 x 1⅜in)
    - For G2 (Zip Pocket Top), cut one piece 20 x 14cm (8 x 5½in)
    - For G3 (Zip Pocket Bottom), cut one piece 20 x 11.5cm (8 x 4½in)

FROM MEDIUM-WEIGHT INTERFACING:

- For A (Main Body), cut two using pattern piece A, cutting on the dotted line
- For B (Gussets), cut four using pattern piece B
- For D (Card Holder), cut three pieces 9.5 x 1.2cm (3¾ x ½in)
- For E (Slip and Lipbalm Pockets), cut one piece 18 x 10.5cm (7 x 4¼in)
- For G (Zip Pocket) – this comprises pieces G1, G2 and G3
    - For G1 (Zip Pocket Facing), cut one piece 20 x 3.5cm (8 x 1⅜in)
    - For G2 (Zip Pocket Top), cut one piece 20 x 14cm (8 x 5½in)
    - For G3 (Zip Pocket Bottom), cut one piece 20 x 11.5cm (8 x 4½in)

FROM DECOVIL 1/PELTEX:

- For A (Main Body), cut one using pattern piece A, cutting on the dotted line

STABILIZERS

1 Following the pattern, cut out the ovals on the interfacing and Decovil/Peltex main body pieces.

2 Fuse medium-weight interfacing to the exterior and lining main body pieces (A), the exterior and lining fabric gussets (B), the slip and lipbalm pockets (E), and all three zip pocket pieces (G). Put the medium-weight interfacing for the card holder (D) to one side.

3 Fuse the Decovil/Peltex to the main body (A) exterior fabric, centring it on the panel.

4 Mark the centres of all pieces within the seam allowance.

LINING CONSTRUCTION

5 Construct the zip pocket (*see Pockets: Hidden Tape Zip Pocket*), making the box on the zip pocket facing 15cm (6in) long. Attach it to the lining main body (A) panel, placing the bottom edge of the zip pocket facing (G1) 10.5cm (4¼in) from the centre of the panel.

6 Construct the all-in-one card holder, slip and lipbalm pocket, using pieces D, E and F and medium-weight interfacing pieces D and E (*see Pockets*). Don't forget to sew this section using a 6mm (¼in) seam allowance. Attach the completed pocket panel to the lining main body (A) panel, placing it 2.5cm (1in) from the centre crease and 1.2cm (½in) from each edge.

7 With right sides together, pin the lining handle facings (C) to the lining main body (A), placing them 16cm (6¼in) from the centre crease. Turn the panel over and, using a very short stitch length, sew around the oval interfacing cut-outs. Steam press the stitches, then trim away the excess fabric inside the ovals using pinking shears or snipping into the seam allowance. Clip into the curve of the ovals without snipping any stitches.

8 Pull the handle facings (C) away from the stitching and press to ensure a neat turn-through. Push the handle facings (C) through the main body (A), then press in place.

9 Insert two magnetic snaps (*see Hardware & Bling: Regular Magnetic Snaps*), placing the centres of the washers 6cm (2⅜in) from each edge and 16cm (6¼in) from the centre crease.

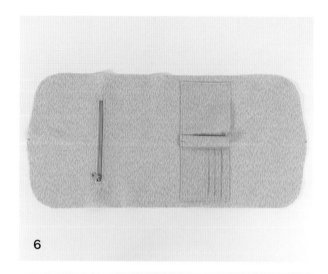

6

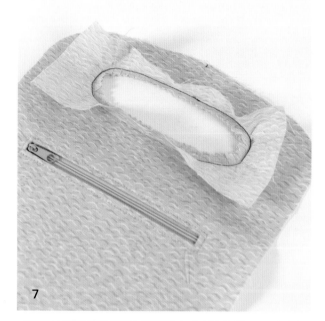

7

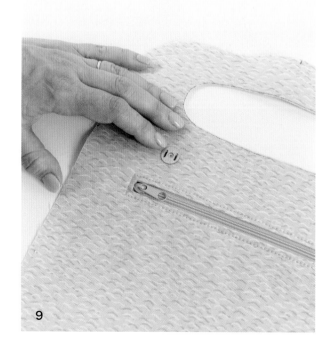

9

Top tip

Using a small stitch length around the handle cut-outs will make it easier to sew the curve accurately.

13

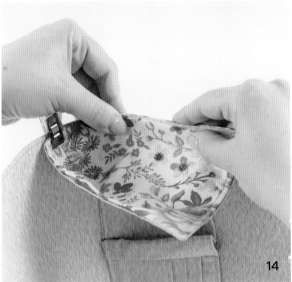

14

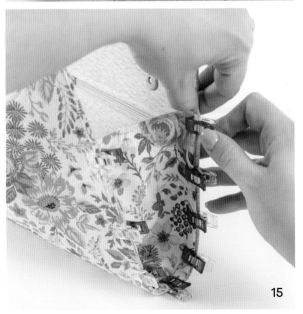

15

EXTERIOR CONSTRUCTION

10 Repeat steps 7 and 8 for the outer handle facings (C).

11 Place the outer and lining main bodies right sides together and sew around the outer edges, leaving a turning gap in one side (*see Professional Touches: Turning Gaps*). Do not sew around the handle cut-outs. Clip the curves or trim with pinking shears.

12 Turn the main body (A) right side out and run a blunt tool such as a crochet hook around all the curves inside to ensure they're fully pushed out. Press well. Match the handle edges, then topstitch around the handle cut-outs 3mm (⅛in) from the edge and then around the entire outside edge of the main body. This will close the turning gap.

FINISH THE BAG

13 Fold each outer and lining gusset (B) right sides together, matching the bottom dart line. Sew along the dart using a 6mm (¼in) seam allowance (*see Shaping: Darts*). Snip into the seam allowance at the centre and finger press the seams open. Place one outer and one lining gusset right sides together, matching the raw edges and the dart. Sew around all edges using a 6mm (¼in) seam allowance, leaving a turning gap in one edge. Clip the corners, then turn right side out. Press well, taking care not to flatten the dart. Repeat for the second gusset (B).

14 Match the finished dart on one gusset (B) to the centre of the main body (A).

15 Pin, then sew the gusset into the main body, manipulating the main body to allow the gusset to be sewn into place with ease. Repeat with the second gusset on the other side of the main body.

The Interchange Crossbody
BACKPACK

The interchange backpack converts easily to a crossbody or shoulder bag by unclipping the strap and attaching it to different rings on the top of the bag. There's a hidden back pocket under the flap for extra security and plenty of scope for adding extra pockets inside. It's a versatile bag and great for a day trip, a business meeting or running errands. Use the flap to showcase a really special print for a bag that you'll love using time and again.

FABRICS USED

Boho Meadow Border by Dashwood, teal faux leather and Boho Meadow Bohemian Geometric by Dashwood

SKILL LEVEL

Advanced beginner

YOU WILL NEED

Fabrics

1m (1⅛yd) exterior fabric plus 10cm x 2.3m (4 x 90in) strap fabric

1 fat quarter contrast fabric

1.5m (1⅝yd) lining fabric

3m (3¼yd) medium-weight interfacing, 90cm (1yd) wide; narrower interfacing will need more

1m (1⅛yd) foam stabilizer, 72cm (28in) wide; narrower stabilizer will need more

NOTE

These amounts are for non-directional fabrics; directional fabrics may need more.

Notions

1 x 20cm (8in) #3 zip to match lining fabric

3 x 25mm (1in) swivel clips

4 x 25mm (1in) triangle rings

1 x 38mm (1½in) O-ring

1 x bridge anchor

1 x 25mm (1in) strap slider

4 x double-cap rivets, 8mm (⁵⁄₁₆in) post x 9mm (³⁄₈in) cap (optional)

FINISHED SIZE (W x H x D)

29 x 27 x 12.5cm (11½ x 10½ x 5in)

Top tip

Why not add a full-width slip pocket to the lining?

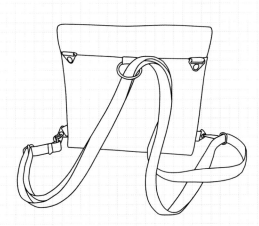

CUTTING INSTRUCTIONS

All measurements are given as width x height. A seam allowance of 1cm (⅜in) is included.

FROM EXTERIOR FABRIC

- For A (Adjustable Strap), cut one piece 10 x 182cm (4 x 72in); you may need to piece this (*see Handles & Straps: To Piece a Strap*)

- For B (Main Panels), cut two pieces using pattern piece B; if you're using a thick fabric, cut one main panel from exterior fabric and one from lining fabric

- For C (Back Pocket), fold pattern piece B along the dotted line, then cut one

- For E (Tabs), cut six pieces 5 x 5cm (2 x 2in)

FROM CONTRAST OR LINING FABRIC

- For D (Flap), cut one piece using pattern piece D

FROM LINING FABRIC

- For B (Main Panels), cut two pieces using pattern piece B

- For C (Back Pocket), fold pattern piece B along the dotted line, then cut one

- For D (Flap), cut one piece using pattern piece D

- For F (Slip and Zip Pockets), cut two pieces 25.5 x 30.5cm (10 x 12in)

FROM MEDIUM-WEIGHT INTERFACING

- For A (Adjustable Strap), cut one piece 10 x 182cm (4 x 72in)

- For B (Main Panels), cut four pieces using pattern piece B

- For C (Back Pocket), fold pattern piece B along the dotted line, then cut two

- For D (Flap), cut two pieces using pattern piece D

- For E (Tabs), cut six pieces 5 x 5cm (2 x 2in)

- For F (Slip and Zip Pockets), cut two pieces 25.5 x 30.5cm (10 x 12in)

FROM FOAM STABILIZER

- For B (Main Panels), rough cut two pieces, then trim after tacking (basting)

- For D (Flap), rough cut one piece, then trim after tacking (basting)

STABILIZERS

1 Fuse medium-weight interfacing to all pieces. Tack (baste) foam stabilizer to the exterior main panels (B) and the contrast flap (D) – *see Tools & Materials: Interfacing and Stabilizers*.

LINING CONSTRUCTION

2 Using the 20cm (8in) #3 zip and one (F) panel, make and insert one zip pocket into one lining main panel (B), making the box 20cm (8in) long and 12.5cm (5in) from the bottom edge of the zip pocket (*see Pockets: Simple Zip Pocket*). Place the bottom edge of the zip pocket 10cm (4in) from the bottom edge of the panel. Don't forget to leave a turning gap in the bottom of the pocket for turning the bag through.

3 Using the remaining (F) panel, make a simple slip pocket (*see Pockets: Simple Slip Pocket*). Attach the slip pocket to the remaining lining main panel (B), placing it 9cm (3½in) from the bottom of the panel and centred on the width. Divide it if you wish (*see Pockets: Divided Slip Pocket*).

4 Place the lining main panels (B) right sides together and sew along the sides and bottom edges, leaving the corner cut-outs open (*see Professional Touches: Well-fitting Linings*).

5 Press open the side and bottom seams, then box the corners (*see Shaping: Cut-out Boxed Corners*).

The lining construction is finished for now and can be placed to one side.

3

5

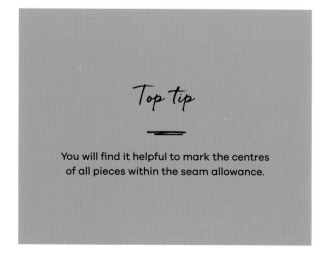

Top tip

You will find it helpful to mark the centres of all pieces within the seam allowance.

6

8

EXTERIOR CONSTRUCTION

6 Fold two raw edges of one tab (E) to the centre and press in place. Topstitch along both folded edges 3mm (⅛in) from the edge. Thread the tab over the bar of a swivel clip and tack (baste) it to the centre of the right side of the contrast flap (D) within the seam allowance.

7 Place the contrast and lining flaps (D) right sides together and sew around the curved edges, leaving the straight top edge open. Clip into the curves and turn right side out. Press well, then topstitch all around the curved edges 3mm (⅛in) from the edge. Tack (baste) along the open straight edge within the seam allowance.

8 Repeat step 6 to make two more tabs (E) with triangle rings attached. Tack (baste) them to the right side of the straight edge of the contrast flap (D), with the edges of the tabs 1.2cm (½in) from the side edges of the flap. Make another tab with an O-ring attached and tack it to the centre of the straight edge of the contrast flap.

9 Place the flap (D) and the exterior back pocket (C) right sides together, matching the centres. Match the straight edge of the flap to the top edge of the back pocket and make sure the tabs hang downwards. Place the lining back pocket right side down on top and sew through all layers along the top edge only.

9

10 Open out and press the flap (D) and exterior back pocket (C) away from the lining back pocket. With the panel opened out, topstitch across the lining back pocket 3mm (⅛in) away from the seam to hold the seam allowances together.

11 Place the open panel, right sides together on top of one exterior main panel (B) matching side and bottom edges (*see Pockets: Full-width Slip Pocket*), following the instructions for a bag with boxed corners.

12 Trim the lining back pocket (C) 6mm (¼in) from the sewn lines to reduce the bulk. Pull the exterior back pocket down, smooth it flat over the sewn lines and tack (baste) around all edges, concealing the sewn lines.

13 If you would like to add rivets, do so now; insert one rivet on each side through the entire back pocket (C), flap (D) and exterior main panel (B), positioning it just below the flap seam and to the right of the edge of the flap.

14 Insert the bridge anchor into the second exterior main panel (B), placing it 8.5cm (3¼in) from the bottom of the panel and centred on the width.

15 Repeat step 6 to make two more tabs (E) with triangle rings attached, stitching them 2cm (¾in) from the bottom corner cut-out on each side of the exterior main panel (B) with pocket attached.

16 Place the exterior main panels (B) right sides together and sew along the side and bottom edges, leaving the corner cut-outs open.

17 Sew the boxed corners (*see Shaping: Cut-out Boxed Corners*).

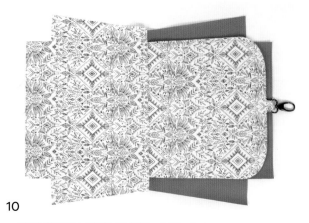

10

12

14

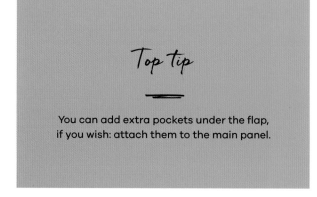

Top tip

You can add extra pockets under the flap, if you wish: attach them to the main panel.

FINISH THE BAG

18 With right sides together, matching the side seams and raw edges, place the exterior bag inside the lining, tucking the flap down inside, out of the way. Sew all around the top. Turn through the gap in the bottom of the zip pocket and then stitch the gap closed.

19 Press the top of the bag well and topstitch all around 3mm (⅛in) from the edge.

20 Make a removable adjustable strap (*see Handles & Straps: Removable Adjustable Strap*), securing the ends with rivets if you wish. Thread the strap through the O-ring and connect it to the bottom tabs to wear as a backpack or to the top tabs to wear as a crossbody bag.

The Darling
DAY SLING

This cute and practical bag is ideal for a day out. With stylish front zip pockets and two exterior slip pockets topped with zip piping, it's incredibly useful – and that's just the outside! Inside, the bag fastens with a zip top and has both zip and slip pockets. You can, of course, customize the interior pockets to suit your own needs.

FABRICS USED

New World Tapestry Little Harlequin by Chatham Glyn, Essex linen in putty and Kona cotton in putty

SKILL LEVEL

Intermediate

YOU WILL NEED

Fabrics

1m (1⅛yd) exterior fabric

1 fat quarter contrast fabric

1m (1⅛yd) lining fabric

1.5m (1¾yd) medium-weight interfacing, 90cm (1yd) wide; narrower interfacing will need more

0.4m (½yd) foam stabilizer, 72cm (28in) wide; narrower stabilizer will need more

NOTE

These amounts are for non-directional fabrics; directional fabrics may need more.

Notions

1 x 15cm (6in) #3 zip to match lining fabric

2 x 15cm (6in) #5 zips to match exterior fabric

1 x 23cm (9in) #5 zip to match lining fabric

1 x 23cm (9in) #5 zip to match exterior fabric to use as piping; trim the tape to 1cm (⅜in) seam allowance

1 x 25mm (1in) rectangle ring

1 x 25mm (1in) strap slider

1 x zip end

FINISHED SIZE (W x H x D)

20 x 26 x 7cm (8 x 10 x 2¾in)

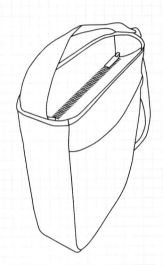

CUTTING INSTRUCTIONS

All measurements are given as width x height. A seam allowance of 1cm (⅜in) is included.

FROM EXTERIOR FABRIC

- For A (Adjustable Strap), cut one piece 10 x 137cm (4 x 54in) and one piece 5 x 12.5cm (2 x 5in); you may need to piece the longer strap (*see Handles & Straps: To Piece a Strap*)

- For B (Main Panels), cut two pieces using pattern piece B

- For D (Gusset), cut one piece 8 x 69cm (3¼ x 27in)

FROM CONTRAST FABRIC

- For C (Contrast Pockets), cut two pieces using pattern piece C

FROM LINING FABRIC

- For B (Main Panels), cut two pieces using pattern piece B

- For C (Contrast Pockets), cut two pieces using pattern piece C

- For D (Gusset), cut one piece 8 x 69cm (3¼ x 27in)

- For E (Zip Bridge), cut two pieces 20 x 7cm (8 x 2¾in)

- For F (Front Zip and Lining Slip Pockets), cut three pieces 18 x 20cm (7 x 8in)

- For G (Lining Zip Pocket), cut one piece 19 x 25.5cm (7½ x 10in)

FROM MEDIUM-WEIGHT INTERFACING

- For A (Adjustable Strap), cut one piece 10 x 137cm (4 x 54in) and one piece 5 x 12.5cm (2 x 5in)

- For B (Main Panels), cut four pieces using pattern piece B

- For C (Contrast Pockets), cut four pieces using pattern piece C

- For D (Gusset), cut two pieces 8 x 69cm (3¼ x 27in)

- For E (Zip Bridge), cut two pieces 20 x 7cm (8 x 2¾in)

- For F (Front Zip and Lining Slip Pockets), cut three pieces 18 x 20cm (7 x 8in)

- For G (Lining Zip Pocket), cut one piece 19 x 25.5cm (7½ x 10in)

FROM FOAM STABILIZER

- For B (Main Panels), rough cut two pieces, then trim after tacking (basting)

- For D (Gusset), rough cut one piece, then trim after tacking (basting)

STABILIZERS

1 Fuse medium-weight interfacing to all pieces. Tack (baste) foam stabilizer to the exterior main panels (B) and the exterior gusset (D) – *see Tools & Materials: Interfacing and Stabilizers*.

LINING CONSTRUCTION

2 Using the 15cm (6in) #3 zip and the lining zip pocket panel (G), make a zip pocket and insert it into one lining main panel (B), making the box 14cm (5½in) long and 10cm (4in) from the bottom of the zip pocket panel (*see Pockets: Simple Zip Pocket*). Place the bottom edge of the zip pocket 6.5cm (2½in) from the bottom edge of the lining panel. Once you've sewn the zip pocket in place, pin it up and out of the way. Don't forget to leave a turning gap in the bottom of the pocket for closing the main turning gap.

3 Using one lining slip pocket (F), make a simple slip pocket (*see Pockets: Simple Slip Pocket*). Attach the slip pocket to the lining main panel (B) that has the zip pocket, placing it 5cm (2in) from the bottom of the main panel and centred on the width. Divide it if you wish (*see Pockets: Divided Slip Pocket*). Then unpin the zip pocket.

4 Using the 23cm (9in) #5 zip, create a zip bridge (*see Zip Closures: Adding a Zip Bridge on top of a Lining*). Attach it to the lining main panels 2cm (¾in) from the top and centred on the width.

5 Attach each lining main panel (B) to the lining gusset (D) – *see Shaping: Gussets* – leaving a sizeable turning gap on one side edge. Due to the small size of this bag, stitch the first and last 2.5cm (1in) on each side using the regular seam allowance of 1cm (⅜in), but increase to 1.2cm (½in) in between (*see Professional Touches: Well-fitting Linings*).

The lining construction is finished for now and can be placed to one side.

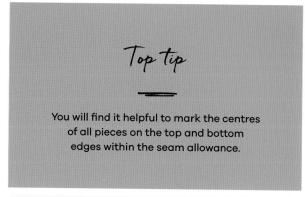

Top tip

You will find it helpful to mark the centres of all pieces on the top and bottom edges within the seam allowance.

4a

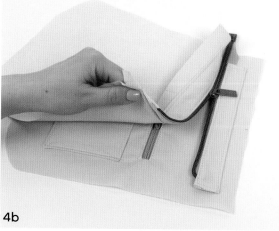

4b

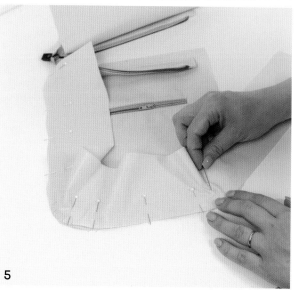

5

EXTERIOR CONSTRUCTION

6 Pin the front zip pockets (F) right side down on the right side of one contrast pocket (C), as indicated on the pattern. Transfer the zip pocket markings onto the wrong side of the fabric (*see Pockets: Simple Zip Pocket*).

7 Sew both pocket boxes, cut along the centre line and corner triangles on each one (*see Pockets: Simple Zip Pocket*) and push through to the wrong side.

8 Using a 15cm (6in) #5 zip, complete the first zip pocket. Pin it out of the way and repeat for the second zip pocket. Then unpin the zip pocket.

9 Trim the end from the 23cm (9in) #5 zip, then pull the two sides apart. Add zip piping to the top edge of the contrast pocket (*see Piping: Using a Zip as Piping*).

10 With right sides together, matching the edges, pin this contrast pocket to one lining contrast pocket and sew along the top edge only. Trim the seam allowance with pinking shears or clip the curves, turn right side out and press well. Topstitch 3mm (⅛in) from the edge.

11 Repeat steps 9 and 10 with the second pair of contrast and lining contrast pockets (C).

12 Place each pair of contrast pockets right side up on an exterior main panel (B), matching the side and bottom edges. Tack (baste) in place.

6

8a

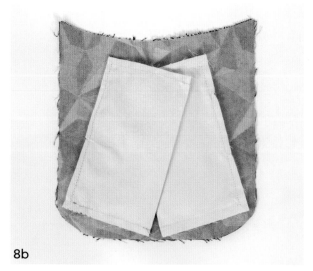

8b

12

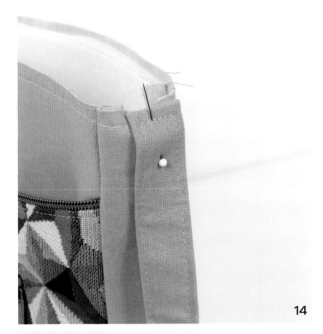

13 With right sides together, attach each exterior main panel (B) to one long edge of the exterior gusset (D) – *see Shaping: Gussets*.

14 Make an adjustable strap (*see Handles & Straps: Fixed Adjustable Strap*). Pin the strap ends right side down to the top of the exterior gusset (D), centred on the width of the gusset, and tack (baste) in place within the seam allowance, making sure the strap is not twisted.

FINISH THE BAG

15 Place the exterior bag inside the lining, right sides together, tucking the strap down inside, out of the way. Sew all around the top edge. Turn through the gap in the side of the lining. Pull the lining through the bottom of the zip pocket and stitch the gap closed, then stitch the bottom of the zip pocket turning gap closed (*see Professional Touches: Turning Gaps*).

16 Press the top of the bag well and topstitch all around 3mm (⅛in) from the edge.

14

The City
TOTE

A sizeable and practical tote, this bag is perfect for transporting work files, folders and all manner of daily belongings. Use it as a baby bag, a gym bag, a school or college bag or even as a shopping bag. The city tote is perfectly adaptable and has a centre zipped divider panel, giving it shape and providing an extra-secure storage pocket.

FABRICS USED

City Nights Multi London Skyline by Lewis and Irene, blue-grey rex faux leather and City Nights Architectural Blender by Lewis and Irene

SKILL LEVEL

Intermediate

YOU WILL NEED

Fabrics

0.5m (⅝yd) exterior fabric

0.75m (⅞yd) faux leather

1.25m (1⅜yd) lining fabric

2m (2¼yd) medium-weight interfacing, 90cm (1yd) wide; narrower interfacing will need more

1m (1⅛yd) foam stabilizer, 72cm (28in) wide; narrower stabilizer will need more

NOTE

These amounts are for non-directional fabrics; directional fabrics may need more.

Notions

1 x 15cm (6in) #3 zip to match lining fabric

1 x 35cm (14in) #5 zip to match lining fabric

1 x 18mm (¾in) slim magnetic snap

4 x diamond strap anchors

1 x rigid bag base, 13 x 33cm (5 x 13in)

6 x 12mm (½in) bag feet

8 x double-cap rivets, 8mm (⁵⁄₁₆in) post x 9mm (⅜in) cap (optional)

FINISHED SIZE (W x H x D)

36 x 27 x 15.5cm (14 x 10½ x 6in)

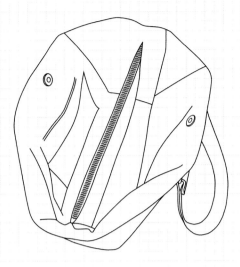

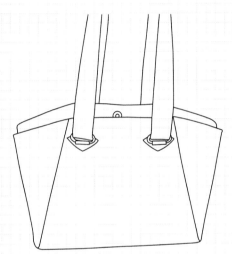

CUTTING INSTRUCTIONS

All measurements are given as width x height. A seam allowance of 1cm (⅜in) is included.

FROM EXTERIOR FABRIC

- For A (Centre Panel), cut two pieces on the fold using pattern piece A

FROM FAUX LEATHER

- For B (End Panels), cut two pieces on the dotted fold line using pattern piece B
- For F (Handles), cut two pieces 13 x 71cm (5 x 28in)

FROM LINING FABRIC

- For A (Centre Panel), cut two pieces using pattern piece A
- For B (End Panels), cut four pieces on the solid line using pattern piece B, with two pieces mirrored
- For C (Zipped Divider), cut four pieces 37.5 x 20cm (14¾ x 8in)
- For D (Slip Pocket), cut one piece 23 x 30.5cm (9 x 12in)
- For E (Zip Pocket) – this comprises pieces E1, E2 and E3
  - E1 (Zip Pocket Facing), cut one piece 20 x 3.5cm (8 x 1⅜in)
  - E2 (Zip Pocket Top), cut one piece 20 x 18cm (8 x 7in)
  - E3 (Zip Pocket Bottom), cut one piece 20 x 15.5cm (8 x 6in)

FROM MEDIUM-WEIGHT INTERFACING

- For A (Centre Panel), cut four pieces using pattern piece A
- For B (End Panels), cut four pieces on the solid line using pattern piece B, with two pieces mirrored
- For C (Zipped Divider), cut four pieces 37.5 x 20cm (14¾ x 8in)
- For D (Slip Pocket), cut one piece 23 x 30.5cm (9 x 12in)
- For E (Zip Pocket) – this comprises pieces E1, E2 and E3
  - E1 (Zip Pocket Facing), cut one piece 20 x 3.5cm (8 x 1⅜in)
  - E2 (Zip Pocket Top), cut one piece 20 x 18cm (8 x 7in)
  - E3 (Zip Pocket Bottom), cut one piece 20 x 15.5cm (8 x 6in)
- For F (Handles), cut two pieces 13 x 71cm (5 x 28in)

FROM FOAM STABILIZER

- For A (Centre Panel), rough cut two pieces, then trim after tacking (basting)
- For B (End Panels), rough cut two pieces, then trim after tacking (basting)

STABILIZERS

1 Fuse medium-weight interfacing to all pieces except the faux leather end panels. Tack (baste) foam stabilizer to both exterior centre panels (A) and both faux leather end panels (B) – *see Tools & Materials: Interfacing and Stabilizers*.

2 Referring to the pattern for placement, punch the holes for the feet and cut slits for the strap anchors in the exterior centre panels. Add a dab of Fray Check to every hole and slit.

LINING CONSTRUCTION

3 Using the 15cm (6in) #3 zip and and the zip pocket panels (E1, E2 and E3), make a zip pocket and insert it into one lining centre panel (A), making the box on the zip facing (E1) 15.5cm (6in) long and placing the top edge of the zip facing 7.5cm (3in) from the top edge of the panel (*see Pockets: Hidden Tape Zip Pocket*). Pin the zip pocket up out of the way for the next step.

4 Make a simple slip pocket, using lining slip pocket (D) – *see Pockets: Simple Slip Pocket*. Attach the slip pocket to the lining centre panel (A) that has the zip pocket, positioning it 10cm (4in) from the bottom of the lining main panel and centred on the width, and dividing it however you choose. Then unpin the zip pocket.

5 With right sides together, matching the tops of each side seam, pin and sew each lining end panel (B) to each side of the lining centre panels (A), stopping at the mark indicated on the pattern piece and leaving a turning gap in one seam. Press the seams open.

6 Attach a magnetic snap to the lining centre panels (A), positioning it 2.5cm (1in) from the top of the panels and centred on the width (*see Hardware & Bling: Regular Magnetic Snaps*).

7 Using the 35cm (14in) #5 zip and panels C and referring to the pattern for placement, insert a zipped divider in each lining centre panel (*see Pockets: Zipped Dividers*).

8 Sew the curved corners by bringing the bottom seam of the lining main panels to match the centre bottom of the end panels (B). Sew with the centre panels on top to prevent any puckering.

The lining construction is finished for now and can be placed to one side.

Top tip

You will find it helpful to mark the centres of all pieces within the seam allowance.

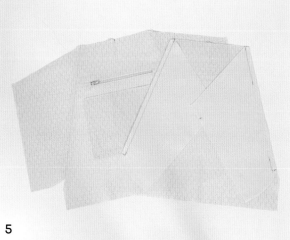

5

EXTERIOR CONSTRUCTION

9 With right sides together, matching the top edges, clip and sew each faux leather end panel (B) between the two exterior centre panels (A), stopping at the mark on the pattern. Press open the seams, then insert the strap anchors using the pre-cut slits.

10 Flatten the panel right sides together, with the two centre panels directly on top of one another, and pin and sew the bottom seam of the exterior centre panels (A).

11 Sew the curved corners, as in step 8.

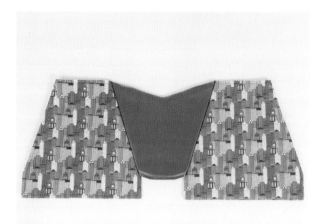

9

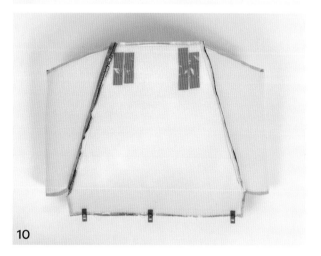

10

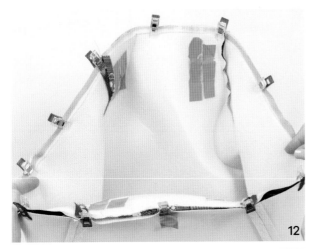

FINISH THE BAG

12 With right sides together, matching the top edges and seams, insert the exterior into the lining section. You will need to manipulate the exterior into place, as it's larger than the lining section. Pin or clip together, then sew around the top edge.

13 Notch the inside corners to ensure a neat finish.

14 Turn the bag right side out, through the gap. Along each long edge of the rigid base, make three holes 2.5cm (1in) in from the edge – one in the centre and one 12.5cm (5in) either side of the centre hole (*see Hardware & Bling: Bag Feet and Solid Bases*). Matching the holes on the base with those on the exterior centre panels, insert the base into the bag, and insert the bag feet.

15 Stitch the turning gap in the side of the lining closed, then tuck the lining down inside the bag. Press the top of the bag well and topstitch around the top 3mm (⅛in) from the edge.

16 Make two handles (G) – *see Handles & Straps: Fully Enclosed Strap*. Thread the handles through the strap anchors by 4cm (1½in) and stitch or rivet in place.

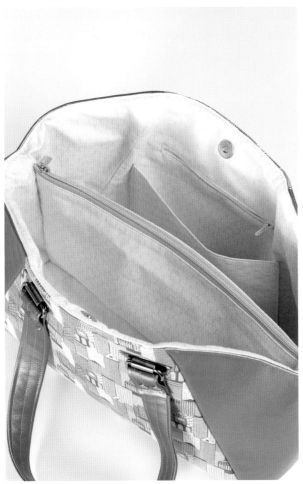

The Criss-Cross
SHOULDER BAG

This sleek shoulder bag is packed full of subtle features. Hidden away inside are pockets galore – a centre zipped divider, slip pockets and a zipped pocket. The exterior is far from boring, with four angled pockets and a great shape to take you from day to night.

FABRICS USED

Black rex faux leather, custom ice dye cotton and coated cotton in putty

SKILL LEVEL

Advanced

YOU WILL NEED

Fabrics

1m (1⅛yd) exterior fabric

2 fat quarters contrast fabric

1.25m (1⅜yd) lining fabric

2m (2¼yd) medium-weight interfacing, 90cm (1yd) wide; narrower interfacing will need more

1m (1⅛yd) foam stabilizer, 72cm (28in) wide; narrower stabilizer will need more

NOTE

These amounts are for non-directional fabrics; directional fabrics may need more.

Avoid faux leather for the exterior fabric unless you have a particularly strong machine.

Notions

1 x 20cm (8in) #3 zip to match lining fabric

1 x 35.5cm (14in) #5 zip to match exterior fabric

1 x 30cm (12in) #5 zip to match lining fabric

1 x rigid bag base, 11.5 x 25.5cm (4½ x 10in)

4 x 12mm (½in) bag feet

2 x 30mm (1¼in) rectangle rings

1 x 30mm (1¼in) strap slider

1 x zip end

FINISHED SIZE (W x H x D)

29 x 26 x 12.5cm (11½ x 10 x 5in)

CUTTING INSTRUCTIONS

All measurements are given as width x height. A seam allowance of 1cm (⅜in) is included.

FROM EXTERIOR FABRIC

- For A (Strap), cut one piece 12.5 x 137cm (5 x 54in) and two pieces 6.5 x 9cm (2½ x 3½in); you may need to piece the long strap (*see Handles & Straps: To Piece a Strap*)

- For B (Main Panels), cut two pieces using pattern piece B

- For C (Zip Bridge), cut four pieces 27 x 3.8cm (10½ x 1½in); if you are using faux leather, cut two from exterior fabric and two from lining fabric to reduce the bulk

- For D (Lining Upper Section), cut two pieces using pattern piece D

FROM CONTRAST FABRIC

- For E (Front Pockets), cut two pieces using pattern piece C with one mirrored. Cut one from each fat quarter

FROM LINING FABRIC

- For E (Front Pockets), cut two pieces using pattern piece E mirrored

- For F (Lining Lower Section), cut two pieces using pattern piece F

- For G (Zipped Divider), cut four pieces 29 x 18cm (11½ x 7in)

- For H (Zip Pocket) – this comprises pieces H1, H2 and H3

  - H1 (Zip Pocket Facing): cut one piece 25.5 x 3.5cm (10 x 1⅜in)

  - H2 (Zip Pocket Top): cut one piece 25.5 x 18cm (10 x 7in)

  - H3 (Zip Pocket Bottom): cut one piece 25.5 x 15cm (10 x 6in)

- For I (Slip Pockets), cut two pieces 25.5 x 30cm (10 x 12in)

FROM MEDIUM-WEIGHT INTERFACING

- For A (Strap), cut one piece 12.5 x 137cm (5 x 54in) and two pieces 6.5 x 9cm (2½ x 3½in)

- For B (Main Panels), cut two pieces using pattern piece B

- For C (Zip Bridge), cut four pieces 27 x 3.8cm (10½ x 1½in)

- For D (Lining Upper Section), cut two pieces using pattern piece D

- For E (Front Pockets), cut four pieces using pattern piece E, with two pieces mirrored

- For F (Lining Lower Section), cut two pieces using pattern piece F

- For G (Zipped Divider), cut four pieces 29 x 18cm (11½ x 7in)

- For H (Zip Pocket) – this comprises pieces H1, H2 and H3

  - H1 (Zip Pocket Facing): cut one piece 25.5 x 3.5cm (10 x 1⅜in)

  - H2 (Zip Pocket Top): cut one piece 25.5 x 18cm (10 x 7in)

  - H3 (Zip Pocket Bottom): cut one piece 25.5 x 15cm (10 x 6in)

- For I (Slip Pockets), cut two pieces 25.5 x 30cm (10 x 12in)

FROM FOAM STABILIZER

- For B (Main Panels), rough cut two pieces, then trim after tacking (basting)

NOTE

If you're using faux leather, you may wish to substitute fusible fleece for the foam stabilizer.

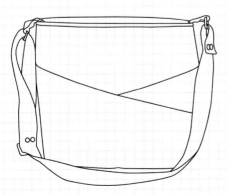

STABILIZERS

1 Fuse medium-weight interfacing to all pieces. Tack (baste) the foam stabilizer to both exterior main panels (B) – *see Tools & Materials: Interfacing and Stabilizers*. Punch the holes for the bag feet (*see Hardware & Bling: Bag Feet and Solid Bases*).

LINING CONSTRUCTION

2 Using the 20cm (8in) #3 zip, make a zip pocket (H) and insert it into one lining lower section (F), making the box on the zip facing (H1) 20cm (8in) long and placing the bottom edge of the zip facing 23cm (9in) from the bottom edge of the panel (*see Pockets: Hidden Tape Zip Pocket*). Don't forget to leave a gap in the bottom of the pocket for turning the bag through. Pin the zip pocket up and out of the way.

3 Make two simple slip pockets, using the lining slip pocket pieces (I) – *see Pockets: Simple Slip Pocket*. Attach a slip pocket to each lining lower section (F), placing it 7.5cm (3in) from the bottom of the panel and centred on the width, and dividing it if you wish. Unpin the zip pocket.

4 Using the 35.5cm (14in) #5 zip, create a zip bridge (*see Zip Closures: Splitting a Lining*). Place it on one lining lower section (F), matching the raw edges and centred on the width, then place a lining upper section (D) right side down on top and stitch through all three layers. Attach the other side of the zip bridge to the other lining upper and lower section panels in the same way. Press the seam allowances towards the lining upper section and topstitch on the lining upper section 3mm (⅛in) from the seam. Add the zip end (*see Hardware & Bling: Metal Zip End*).

5 Using the 30cm (12in) #5 zip and panels (G), make a zipped divider and attach it to the lining main panels using placement mark on the pattern piece (*see Pockets: Zipped Dividers*).

6 Box the corners (*see Shaping: Cut-out Boxed Corners*).

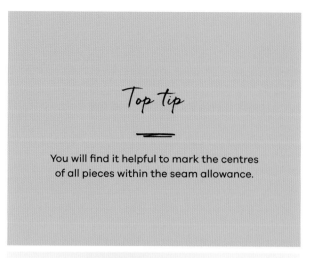

Top tip

You will find it helpful to mark the centres of all pieces within the seam allowance.

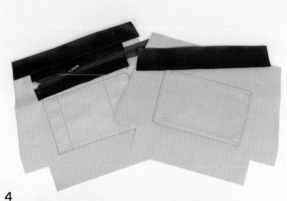

4

EXTERIOR CONSTRUCTION

7 With right sides together, pin and sew each contrast front pocket (E) to its corresponding lining piece along the top edge only. Turn right side out, press and topstitch 3mm (⅛in) from the top edge.

8 Open out one contrast front pocket (E) that will form the back pocket and lay it right side up. Place the second front pocket (which will form the front pocket) on top, also right side up, matching the bottom edges. Roll the second pocket down and pin it out of the way.

9 Pull the bottom edge of the first pocket lining down to match the bottom edge of the second pocket and sew through all four layers.

10 Turn the front pockets (E) right side out through the side opening and press. Topstitch the top edges of both pockets. Place on one exterior main panel (B) 1.5cm (⅝in) from the top of the corner cut-outs and tack (baste) in place along each side. Topstitch along the bottom and up the centre to divide the pockets into four.

11 Sew both exterior main panels (B) together along the side and bottom edges. Box the corners (*see Shaping: Cut-out Boxed Corners*). Turn right side out.

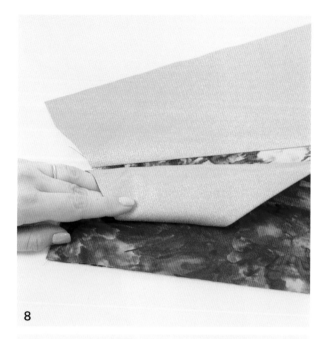

8

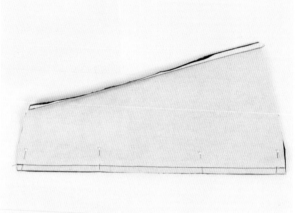

9

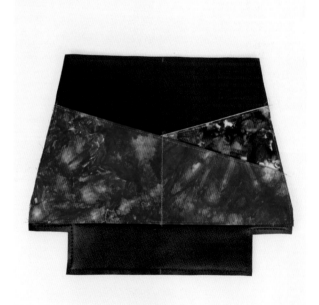

10

12

FINISH THE BAG

12 Using the 6.5 x 9cm (2½ x 3½in) strap pieces (A), make two tabs (*see Handles & Straps: Fixed Adjustable Strap*) with a rectangle ring on each. Centring them over the side seams and matching the raw edges, pin and tack (baste) one tab to the top of each exterior main panel, stitching within the seam allowance.

13 With right sides together, place the exterior bag inside the lining in the section of the lining with the zip pocket turning gap. Sew all around the top of the bag, then turn right side out through the turning gap.

14 Insert the bag base through the turning gap. Through the holes you punched in step 1, mark where to punch holes on the bag base. Remove the base, make the holes, and then insert the base into the bag again. Add the bag feet (*see Hardware & Bling: Bag Feet and Solid Bases*).

15 Stitch the turning gap in the bottom of the zip pocket closed, then tuck the lining down inside the bag. Press the top of the bag well and topstitch around the top 3mm (⅛in) from the edge.

16 Using the 12.5 x 137cm (5 x 54in) strap piece (A), make and attach an adjustable strap (*see Handles & Straps*).

Top tip

———

Decide which of your contrast pocket fabrics you want to cover the full width of the bag exterior and use that as the second front pocket in step 8.

The Trio
POCKETBOOK

This bag is perfect for anyone who loves an organized accessory! The small size belies its usefulness: with three compartments, a zip pocket, slip pocket and removable crossbody strap, you'll love going minimal!

FABRICS USED

Birdie Collection Bird Meet in Navy by Mia Charro, tan rex faux leather and Under the Oak Tree Clover on Cream by Lewis and Irene

SKILL LEVEL

Advanced

YOU WILL NEED

Fabrics

0.5m (⅝yd) faux leather (exterior fabric)

1 fat quarter contrast fabric

0.75m (⅞yd) lining fabric

2m (2¼yd) medium-weight interfacing, 90cm (1yd) wide; narrower interfacing will need more

0.5m (⅝yd) fusible fleece, 72cm (28in) wide; narrower fleece will need more

NOTE

These amounts are for non-directional fabrics; directional fabrics may need more.

Notions

1 x 20cm (8in) #3 zip to match lining fabric; cut the zip teeth down to 22.5cm (8⅞in) long

1 x 18mm (¾in) slim magnetic snap

1 x 23cm (9in) #5 zip to match exterior fabric

6 x double-cap rivets, 8mm (⁵⁄₁₆in) post x 9mm (⅜in) cap

2 x 25mm (1in) triangle rings

2 x 25mm (1in) swivel clips

1 x 25mm (1in) strap slider

FINISHED SIZE (W x H x D)

25.5 x 18 x 6cm (10 x 7 x 2½in)

CUTTING INSTRUCTIONS

All measurements are given as width x height. A seam allowance of 1cm (⅜in) is included.

FROM EXTERIOR FABRIC

- For A (Strap), cut one piece 10 x 137cm (4 x 54in) and two pieces 5 x 10cm (2 x 4in)

- For B (Main Panels), cut two pieces using pattern piece B

- For C (Centre Panels), cut two pieces using pattern piece C

FROM CONTRAST FABRIC

- For D (Flap), cut one piece using pattern piece D

- For G (Zip Tabs), cut two pieces 3 x 5cm (1¼ x 2in)

FROM LINING FABRIC

- For B (Main Panels), cut two pieces using pattern piece B

- For C (Centre Panels), cut two pieces using pattern piece C

- For D (Flap), cut one piece using pattern piece D

- For E (Slip Pocket), cut one piece 25.5 x 25.5cm (10 x 10in)

- For F (Zip Pocket) – this comprises pieces F1, F2 and F3

  - F1 (Zip Pocket Facing), cut one piece 25.5 x 3.5cm (10 x 1⅜in)

  - F2 (Zip Pocket Top), cut one piece 25.5 x 15cm (10 x 6in)

  - F3 (Zip Pocket Bottom), cut one piece 25.5 x 13cm (10 x 5in)

FROM MEDIUM-WEIGHT INTERFACING

- For A (Strap), cut one piece 10 x 137cm (4 x 54in) and two pieces 5 x 10cm (2 x 4in)

- For B (Main Panels), cut two pieces using pattern piece B

- For C (Centre Panels), cut two pieces using pattern piece C

- For D (Flap), cut one piece using pattern piece D

- For E (Slip Pocket), cut one piece 25.5. x 25.5cm (10 x 10in)

- For F (Zip Pocket) – this comprises pieces F1, F2 and F3

  - F1 (Zip Pocket Facing), cut one piece 25.5 x 3.5cm (10 x 1⅜in)

  - F2 (Zip Pocket Top), cut one piece 25.5 x 15cm (10 x 6in)

  - F3 (Zip Pocket Bottom), cut one piece 25.5 x 13cm (10 x 5in)

FROM FUSIBLE FLEECE

- For B (Main Panels), cut two pieces using the dotted line on pattern piece B

- For C (Centre Panels), cut two pieces using the dotted line on pattern piece C

- For D (Flap), cut one piece using the dotted line on pattern piece D

NOTE

If you are not using faux leather for the bag exterior, apply interfacing rather than fusible fleece to pieces B and C.

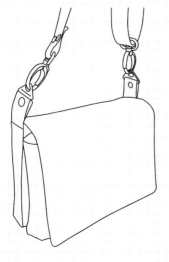

Top tip

Why not add the All-in-One Card Holder, Slip and Lipbalm Pocket from the Pockets section?

STABILIZERS

1 Fuse medium-weight interfacing to all pieces.

2 Fuse fusible fleece to the exterior main panels (B), the exterior centre panels (C) and the contrast flap panel (D).

LINING CONSTRUCTION

3 Using the 20cm (8in) #3 zip and the zip pocket panels (F1, F2 and F3), make a zip pocket and insert it into one lining main panel (B), making the box on the zip facing (F1) 20cm (8in) long and placing the bottom edge of the zip facing 14cm (5½in) from the bottom edge of the panel (*see Pockets: Hidden Tape Zip Pocket*). Don't forget to leave a gap in the bottom of the pocket for turning the bag through.

4 Make a simple slip pocket, using lining slip pocket (E) – *see Pockets: Simple Slip Pocket*. Attach the slip pocket to the second lining main panel (B), placing it 4cm (1½in) from the bottom of the panel and centred on the width, dividing it however you choose.

5 Sew the darts of the lining main panels (B), stitching from the wide end of the dart to the point, using a 6mm (¼in) seam allowance (*see Shaping: Darts*).

6 With right sides together, matching the side and bottom edges, sew the lining main panel with the zip pocket (B) to one lining centre panel (C). You will need to fold each dart to one side and manipulate the edges in order to match them. This piece will now be called the lining pouch and will be used again at the end of construction. Put the other lining panels to one side for now.

Top tip

You will find it helpful to mark the centres of all pieces within the seam allowance.

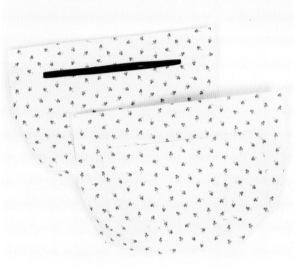

5

6

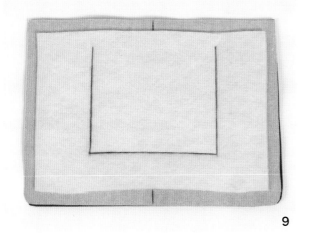

9

10

11

EXTERIOR CONSTRUCTION

7 Attach the female half of the magnetic snap to the right side of one exterior main panel (B), centred on the width and with the bottom of the snap 7.5cm (3in) from the bottom (*see Hardware & Bling: Regular Magnetic Snaps*).

8 Sew the darts of the exterior main panels (B), stitching from the wide end of the dart to the point, using a 6mm (¼in) seam allowance.

9 With right sides together, sew the exterior centre panels (C) together along the dotted line, as indicated on the pattern piece. Backstitch at the start and end of the stitching to reinforce, as this is a stress point.

10 Fold each zip tab in half widthwise, open it out and then fold the two raw edges in to the centre crease and press. Fold in half along the centre crease again and press. Slot the end of the #5 zip into the centre fold and topstitch it in place. Repeat for the other end of the zip. The zip should measure 22.5cm (8⅞in) when both zip tabs have been added.

11 Pin one exterior centre panel (C) down out of the way and apply a line of double-sided basting tape to the right side of the top edge of the second centre panel. Place one edge of the #5 zip right side down on top of the tape, matching the centres, then apply another line of basting tape to the top edge of the zip tape. Pin or clip the remaining lining centre panel right side down on top and sew along the top edge through all three layers, using the regular 1cm (⅜in) seam allowance. Do not topstitch at this stage.

Top tip

—

Using basting tape ensures that zips don't slip out of place while you're sewing.

12 Sandwich the second side of the zip between the exterior main panel with the female half of the snap and the lining main panel with the slip pocket, and sew as before.

13 Open out the zip panel and press, then topstitch around all four edges of the zip to keep the fabric away from the zip teeth. Open the zip.

14 Matching the raw edges, pin or clip the exterior panels to each other, right sides together. Do the same thing with the lining panels. The main panels are larger than the centre panels, so will need to be manipulated into place. Sew around all sides, leaving a turning gap in the bottom of the lining panels.

15 Turn the panel right side out through the turning gap in the bottom of the lining and stitch the turnng gap closed.

16 Fold the zipped front section out of the way. With right sides together, matching the edges, pin the second exterior main panel (B) to the remaining centre panel (C), then sew around the side and bottom edges.

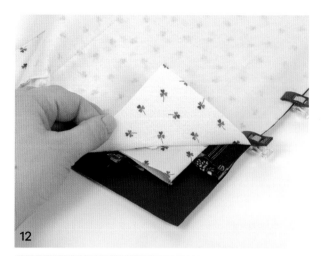

12

13

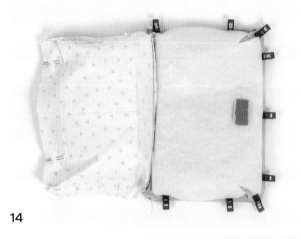

14

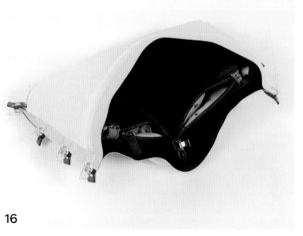

16

19

20

FINISH THE BAG

17 Attach the male half of the magnetic snap to the right side of the lining flap (D), placing the edge of the snap 2.5cm (1in) from the bottom edge of the lining flap and centred on the width.

18 Place the lining and contrast flaps (D) right sides together and sew around the sides, leaving the top straight edge open. Clip the curves and turn the flap right side out. Press well, then topstitch all around 3mm (⅛in) from the edge. Matching the raw edges, place the flap right side down on the exterior main panel (B), centred on the width, and tack (baste) it in place within the seam allowance.

19 Using the 10 x 137cm (4 x 54in) strap piece (A), strap slider and swivel clips, make an adjustable strap (*see Handles & Straps: Removable Adjustable Strap*). If you wish, add a rivet at each stitching line to secure (*see Hardware & Bling: Rivets*). To make the strap tabs, fold the long raw edges of the 10cm (4in) strap pieces in to the centre and topstitch along both long edges. Feed each one over a triangle ring and secure with a rivet. Stitching within the seam allowance, tack (baste) the short straps to the edge of the exterior main panels, next to the flap.

20 With the lining pouch right side out and the exterior of the bag wrong side out, place the lining pouch inside the bag, matching the top edges. Tuck the flap (D) and strap (A) down inside the bag, then sew all around the top edge, manoeuvring the rest of the bag out of the way as necessary.

21 Turn the bag right side out through the turning gap, press the top seam and then topstitch the open pouch side of the bag 3mm (⅛in) from the edge. Sew the turning gap closed.

The Explorer
CARRY-ON

For overnight stays and weekends away,
the Explorer Carry-on is your perfect travel
companion. Big enough for a few days' clothing,
yet small enough to pop on an overhead rack,
this sizeable bag has interior pockets to keep
your accessories organized and exterior pockets
for easy access to items on the go. Practical and
modern, it features two carry handles as well as
a removable adjustable shoulder strap.

FABRICS USED

Tattooed North Sand Dark Grey and Starlight Grey with Gold Metallic

SKILL LEVEL

Advanced

YOU WILL NEED

Fabrics

2m (2¼yd) exterior fabric

2m (2¼yd) lining fabric

4m (4½yd) medium-weight interfacing, 90cm (1yd) wide; narrower interfacing will need more

1.5m (1¾yd) foam stabilizer, 72cm (28in) wide; narrower stabilizer will need more

NOTE

These amounts are for non-directional fabrics; directional fabrics may need an extra 0.5m (½yd).

Notions

0.6m (¾yd) elastic, 1cm (⅜in) wide

2 x 18mm (¾in) magnetic snaps

1 x 25.5cm (10in) #3 zip to match lining fabric

1 x 17.5cm (7in) #3 or #5 zip to match exterior fabric

1 x 66cm (26in) #5 zip to match exterior fabric

86cm (34in) of 8mm (⁵⁄₁₆in) plastic tubing

6 x double-cap rivets, 8mm (⁵⁄₁₆in) post x 9mm (⅜in) cap

6 x 18mm (¾in) bag feet

1 x foam core board, 43 x 20cm (17 x 7¾in)

2 x 25mm (1in) triangle rings

2 x 38mm (1½in) swivel clips

1 x 38mm (1½in) strap slider

FINISHED SIZE (W x H x D)

50 x 35.5 x 22cm (20 x 14 x 9in)

CUTTING INSTRUCTIONS

All measurements are given as width x height. A 1cm (⅜in) seam allowance is included. All fabric pieces are interfaced for extra strength.

FROM EXTERIOR FABRIC:

- For A (Passport Pocket), cut one piece 20 x 20cm (8 x 8in) and one piece 20 x 15cm (8 x 6in)

- For B (Adjustable Strap), cut one piece 15 x 152cm (6 x 60in) and two pieces 5 x 5cm (2 x 2in)

- For C (Rolled Handles), cut two pieces 7 x 106cm (2¾ x 42in)

- For D (Base Gusset), cut one piece 24 x 96.5cm (9½ x 38in)

- For E (Zip Gusset), cut two pieces 12.5 x 61cm (5 x 24in)

- For F (Main Body), cut two using pattern piece F

- For G (Slip Pockets), cut one using pattern piece G

FROM LINING FABRIC:

- For A (Passport Pocket), cut one piece 20 x 20cm (8 x 8in) and one piece 20 x 15cm (8 x 6in)

- For D (Base Gusset), cut one piece 24 x 96.5cm (9½ x 38in)

- For E (Zip Gusset), cut two pieces 12.5 x 61cm (5 x 24in)

- For F (Main Body), cut two using pattern piece F

- For G (Slip Pockets), cut three using pattern piece G

- For H (Elasticated Pocket), cut two using pattern piece H

- For I (Gusset Pocket), cut two using pattern piece I

- For J (Zip Pocket) – this comprises pieces J1, J2 and J3

  - J1 (Zip Pocket Facing), cut one piece 31 x 3.5cm (12 x 1⅜in)

  - J2 (Zip Pocket Top), cut one piece 31 x 23cm (12 x 9in)

  - J3 (Zip Pocket Bottom), cut one piece 31 x 20cm (12 x 8in)

Top tip

You will find it helpful to mark the centres of all pieces on the top and bottom edges within the seam allowance.

FROM MEDIUM-WEIGHT INTERFACING:

- For A (Passport Pocket), cut two pieces 20 x 20cm (8 x 8in) and two pieces 20 x 15cm (8 x 6in)

- For B (Adjustable Strap), cut one piece 15 x 152cm (6 x 60in) and two pieces 5 x 5cm (2 x 2in)

- For C (Rolled Handles), cut two pieces 7 x 106cm (2¾ x 42in)

- For D (Base Gusset), cut two pieces 24 x 96.5cm (9½ x 38in)

- For E (Zip Gusset), cut four pieces 12.5 x 61cm (5 x 24in)

- For F (Main Body), cut four using pattern piece F

- For G (Slip Pockets), cut four using pattern piece G

- For H (Elasticated Pocket), cut one using pattern piece H

- For I (Gusset Pocket), cut one using pattern piece I

- For J (Zip Pocket) – this comprises pieces J1, J2 and J3

  - For J1 (Zip Pocket Facing), cut one piece 31 x 3.5cm (12 x 1⅜in)

  - For J2 (Zip Pocket Top), cut one piece 31 x 23cm (12 x 9in)

  - For J3 (Zip Pocket Bottom), cut one piece 31 x 20cm (12 x 8in)

FROM FOAM STABILIZER:

- For D (Base Gusset), rough cut one, attach to exterior piece, then trim after tacking (basting)

- For E (Zip Gusset), rough cut two, attach to exterior pieces, then trim after tacking (basting)

- For F (Main Body), rough cut two, attach to exterior pieces, then trim after tacking (basting)

- For G (Slip Pockets), rough cut two, attach to one exterior slip pocket and one lining slip pocket, then trim after tacking (basting)

STABILIZERS

1 Fuse medium-weight interfacing to all passport pocket pieces (A), all adjustable strap pieces (B), both rolled handles (C), the exterior base gusset (D), all zip gussets (E), all main bodies (F), all slip pockets (G), one elasticated pocket (H), one gusset pocket (I) and all zip pocket pieces (J1, J2 and J3).

2 Tack (baste) foam stabilizer to the exterior base gusset (D), both exterior zip gussets (E), both exterior main body pieces (F), one exterior slip pocket (G) and one lining slip pocket (G).

LINING CONSTRUCTION

3 Using two lining slip pockets (G) and a magnetic snap, assemble a full-width slip pocket (*see Pockets: Full-width Slip Pocket*). Matching the side and bottom edges, pin the pocket to the right side of one lining main body panel (F). Tack (baste) in place within the seam allowance (the second pair of slip pockets will be used later).

4 Using the 25.5cm (10in) #3 zip and the zip pocket pieces (J2 and J3), make a zip pocket and insert it into the second lining main body panel (F), making the box on the zip facing (J1) 25.5cm (10in) from the bottom edge of the panel (*see Pockets: Hidden Tape Zip Pocket*). Don't forget to leave a gap in the bottom of the pocket for turning the bag through.

5 Make an elasticated pocket (H) – *see Pockets: Elasticated Pocket for a Panel*, cutting the elastic 24cm (9½in) long. Attach it to the right side of the lining main body panel with the zip pocket, placing it 2.5cm (1in) from the bottom raw edge.

6 Make the gusset pocket (I) cutting the elastic 24cm (9½in) long. Place it on the lining base gusset (D), 2.5cm (1in) from the top of the base gusset (*see Pockets: Elasticated Pocket Sewn into Side Seams*).

5

6

EXTERIOR CONSTRUCTION

7 Apply a line of double-sided basting tape along the bottom edge of the smaller exterior passport pocket (A), on the right side of the fabric. Matching the raw edges, with the zip pull to the left, place the 17.5cm (7in) #3 or #5 zip right side down on top. Apply another line of double-sided basting tape on top, then place the matching lining panel right side down on top of that, again matching the raw edges. Sew using a 6mm (¼in) seam allowance for a #3 zip and a 1cm (⅜in) seam allowance for a #5 zip, then turn wrong sides together and press the fabric away from the zip. Topstitch 3mm (⅛in) from the edge. Attach the remaining passport pocket pieces to the other side of the zip in the same way.

8 Fold the passport pocket right sides together, matching exterior to exterior and lining to lining. You will have a stack of two lining pieces right sides together and two exterior pieces right sides together. Match the bottom raw edges of the exterior to the bottom raw edges of the lining and sew along this edge only, through all four layers, using a 6mm (¼in) seam allowance.

9 Turn right side out and press, with the seam centred on the bottom, then topstitch both the top and bottom edges. Pin the passport pocket to the right side of one exterior main body (F), positioning it 6cm (2½in) from the bottom edge, and sew in place along the raw side edges only, using a 6mm (¼in) seam allowance. This will form a sleeve for the bag to be placed over a suitcase handle.

10 Cut the plastic tubing into two 43cm (17in) lengths. Construct the rolled handles (C) (*see Handles & Straps: Rolled Handles*), sewing 30.5cm (12in) from each end to create a rolled section 45.5cm (18in) long, using a 2mm (scant ⅛in) seam allowance

11 Place one rolled handle over the main body panel that has the passport pocket attached. Place the bottom raw edges on the bottom raw edge of the main body (F) and position them 9cm (3½in) from the centre mark. There should be 18cm (7in) between them; this will hide the raw edges of the passport pocket. Topstitch them in place: start 1.5mm (¹⁄₁₆in). from the bottom, then stitch up for 28cm (11in), across the top and down the second side.

12 Add two rivets (*see Hardware & Bling: Rivets*) to the centre of each side of the handle, placing them 1.5cm (⅝in) above and 1.2cm (½in) below the stitching line. Attach the second rolled handle to the second main body panel in the same way, adding two rivets to each side.

13 Construct a second full-width slip pocket (G) using the exterior slip pocket, remaining lining slip pocket and a magnetic snap and tack (baste) it over the rolled handles on the right side of the second main body panel (F).

7

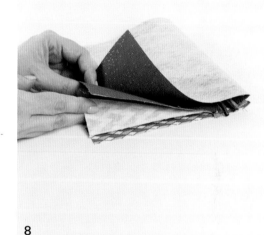

8

11

Top tip

If you would like to add piping to the bag, pull the lining gusset out of the way and apply the piping all the way around the outer gusset after step 16.

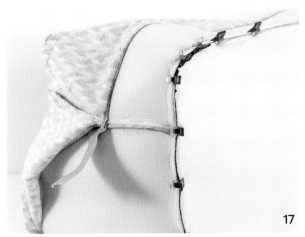

FINISH THE BAG

14 Make six holes for the bag feet (*see Hardware & Bling: Bag Feet and Solid Bases*) in the exterior base gusset (D) placing them 4cm (1½in) from the long edge with one in the centre and and the other two 20cm (8in) either side of it. Make matching holes in the foam core board, 1cm (⅜in) from each edge.

15 Using the 5 x 5cm (2 x 2in) side tab pieces (B), make two tabs with a triangle ring on each (*see Handles & Straps: Fixed Adjustable Strap*). Place each tab on the base gusset (D), with the raw edge of the tabs overhanging the short edge of the gusset by 1.5cm (⅝in), then tack (baste) in place.

16 Construct the zip gusset, using zip gussets (E) and base gusset (D) with the 66cm (26in) #5 zip (*see Zip Closures: Zip Gusset Closure*).

17 Attach each main body (F) panel to the relevant gusset edge. Attach the lining panels first, then the outer panels. Sew the seam allowances of the main panels together at the top to ensure that the lining doesn't sag into the bag when it's full. Turn right side out through the gap in the zip pocket.

18 Reach through the turning gap in the zip pocket and insert the foam core board base and bag feet (*see Hardware & Bling: Bag Feet and Solid Bases*).

19 Finally, make the adjustable strap (B); (*see Handles & Straps: Removable Adjustable Strap*). Clip the strap onto the triangle rings and you're good to go!

About the author

Author photo by Our Beautiful Adventure

Samantha Hussey, or Mrs H to her fans, is a bag patterns designer based in the beautiful Welsh Valleys with her husband Dus and her unfortunately nicknamed daughter, Elvis.

Samantha was diagnosed with dyslexia during high school and has fought to overcome any idiosyncrasies that would otherwise prevent her from writing a book such as this. In 2011 she discovered that her dyslexia allows her to see 3D forms in their 2D components and has since enjoyed finding a niche where her diagnosis is a gift rather than a hindrance.

As well as having her own line of contemporary bag sewing patterns on her website, www.mrs-h.com, Samantha hosts The Bag Retreat, a bag making getaway for sewists. She also runs The Bag of the Month Club, a bag patterns subscription club, with leading Canadian designer and fellow author Janelle MacKay of Emmaline Bags. Samantha has worked with some of the top brands in the industry, including Emmaline Bags, Janome and Mettler.

Acknowledgements

I could not have written this book without the love and encouragement from my husband Dus and our daughter Cicely. Thank you for believing in me, for bringing me food at my cutting table and for being patient when deadlines are looming.

I am so blessed and fortunate to be able to thank my local church family for supporting my endeavours, both at Hope Church Cwmaman and at Freedom in Christ Ladies Group. You have truly made this book possible with your friendship, support and, at times, childcare.

Great thanks to my testing team, who find my every error and fault and then gently and sensitively correct them. I would not be the designer I am today without your guidance and advice.

Special thanks to my sisters Amanda and Lizzie, who both support my business and work with me to ensure the best customer experience that we can imagine. Thanks to Moira, Pete and Lynne for helping us to run Sewing Patterns by Mrs H with such efficiency.

Thanks to the team at David and Charles, who have guided me through this process to produce a book that I am inordinately proud of. Thanks to Sarah C for seeing my potential, to Jessica for keeping me on track, to Jason for taking the most beautiful photograph I've ever seen of a zipped gusset and to Sarah H for ensuring that this book is the best it can be with kindness and encouragement. Thank you also to Blueriver Cottages (www.bluerivercottages.co.uk) for letting us hire your location for the photoshoots.

A special mention to Ben James for creating the line drawn graphics throughout and turning my hand-drawn pattern pieces into something that others would be able to interpret. Thank you for your patience when I couldn't communicate what was needed, and for your haste when time was marching on without me.

Thanks to Luke and Rob for keeping me sewing and to Katie and the girls for helping me to be the best version of me that I can be.

Finally, thanks to Cyndi and Janelle for the messages at 2 a.m. telling me to go to bed, for the down-to-earth advice through every day and for reminding me that I am enough.

Sponsors

Thanks to the generosity of Janome UK, I use a Janome HD9 straight stitch sewing machine. There is nothing I would like to change about this machine, except for the addition of a handy secret snacks compartment!

Many thanks to Janelle from Emmaline Bags for providing the hardware and bling required to share the techniques and projects in this book. The quality of her hardware can only be rivalled by her customer service, both of which are exceptional.

Finally thanks to Rebecca, Pam and the team at Sew Hot – firstly for providing the beautiful fabrics used throughout this book, and secondly for not laughing when I have to make duplicate orders from not reading my own instructions accurately... it's almost as though they have grown used to my failings!

Here are some of the most popular fabric and bag making suppliers.

SUPPLIERS OF FABRICS AND HARDWARE USED IN THIS BOOK

CUSTOM HAND-DYED COTTON

Purple Stitches
www.purple-stitches.com/shop

ALL OTHER FABRICS

Sew Hot
www.sewhot.co.uk

ALL HARDWARE

Emmaline Bags
www.emmalinebags.com

GENERAL FABRICS

The Eternal Maker
www.eternalmaker.com

The Little Kraft Shed
www.thelittlekraftshed.co.uk

The Log Cabin
www.logcabin-billericay.co.uk

Nimble Thimbles
www.nimblethimbles.co.uk

Wool Warehouse
www.woolwarehouse.co.uk/fabric

Sewilicious
www.sewiliciousfabrics.co.uk

Doughty's
www.doughtysonline.co.uk

SPECIALIST FABRICS – HARRIS TWEED, CORK AND FAUX LEATHER

Fabric Online
www.fabric-online.co.uk

Tweed Authority
www.harristweed.org/buy-harris-tweed

The Little British Fabric Shop
www.thelittlebritishfabricshop.co.uk

A Rainbow of Stitches
www.a-rainbow-of-stitches.co.uk

The Yorkshire Fabric Shop
www.yorkshirefabricshop.com

HARDWARE AND GENERAL BAG MAKING SUPPLIES

Betty Box Pleat
www.bettybp.com.au

Emmaline Bags
www.emmalinebags.com

Sew Hot
www.sewhot.co.uk

Sewcial Studio
www.thesewcialstudio.co.uk

2 Minutes 2 Stitch
www.etsy.com/uk/shop/2Minutes2Stitch

THREADS, NOTIONS AND ZIPS

Empress Mills
www.empressmills.co.uk

Hobbycraft
Nationwide stores
www.hobbycraft.co.uk

Jaycotts
www.jaycotts.co.uk

Zipper Station
www.zipperstation.co.uk

Pattern Index

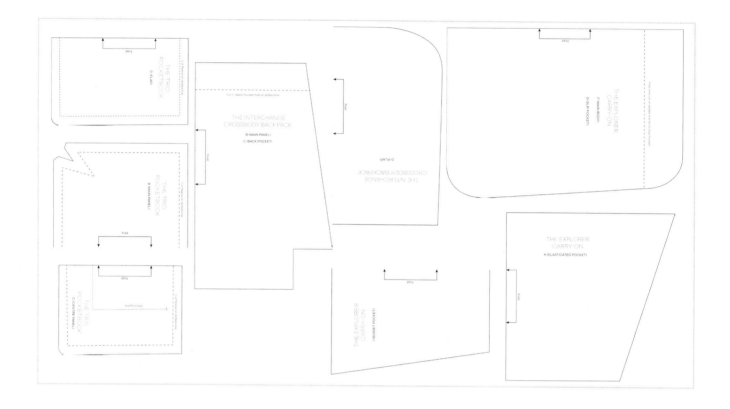

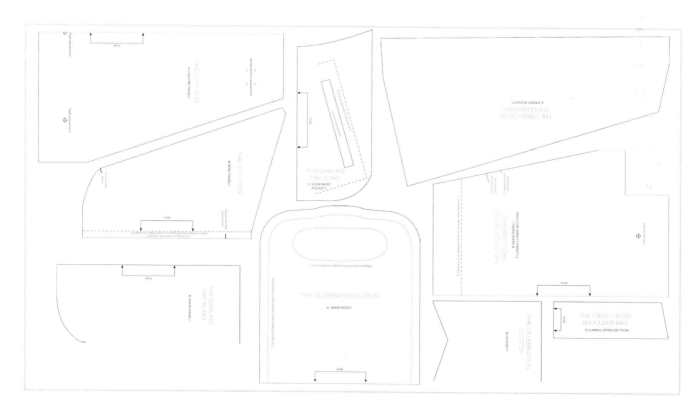

Index

For Dus & Elvis, the light in my everyday

A DAVID AND CHARLES BOOK
© David and Charles, Ltd 2020

David and Charles is an imprint of David and Charles, Ltd
1 Emperor Way, Exeter Business Park, Exeter, EX1 3QS

Text and Designs © Samantha Hussey 2020
Layout and Photography © David and Charles, Ltd 2020

First published in the UK and USA in 2020

ISBN-13: 9781446308110 paperback
ISBN-13: 9781446379615 EPUB

Printed in China by Asia Pacific for:
David and Charles, Ltd
1 Emperor Way, Exeter Business Park, Exeter, EX1 3QS

10 9 8 7 6 5 4 3 2 1

Publishing Director: Ame Verso
Senior Commissioning Editor: Sarah Callard
Managing Editors: Jeni Hennah and Jessica Cropper
Project Editor: Sarah Hoggett
Design Manager: Anna Wade
Art Direction: Prudence Rogers
Photographer: Jason Jenkins
Production Manager: Beverley Richardson

David and Charles publishes high-quality books on a wide range of subjects. For more information visit www.davidandcharles.com.

Layout of the digital edition of this book may vary depending on reader hardware and display settings.